刘谦功 **主编**

刘谦功 舒燕 于洁 **编著**

文化欣赏读本《下》
汉英对照

Exploring Chinese Culture
A CHINESE READER II

北京语言大学出版社
BEIJING LANGUAGE AND CULTURE
UNIVERSITY PRESS

中央广播电视大学音像出版社
MULTIMEDIA PRESS, OPEN UNIVERSITY OF CHINA

图书在版编目(CIP)数据

中国文化欣赏读本. 下：汉英对照 / 刘谦功主编；
舒燕，于洁编著. -- 北京：北京语言大学出版社，
2014.6（2022.10 重印）

ISBN 978-7-5619-3679-5

Ⅰ.① 中... Ⅱ.① 刘... ② 舒燕... ③ 于... Ⅲ.① 汉语—
对外汉语教学—语言读物 ②中华文化—基本知识—汉语、
英语 Ⅳ.①H195.5 ②K203

中国版本图书馆CIP数据核字(2014)第079442号

BLCUP

书　　名	中国文化欣赏读本. 下. 汉英对照
	ZHONGGUO WENHUA XINSHANG DUBEN. XIA. HAN YING DUIZHAO
中文编辑	李佳琳
英文翻译	孙齐圣　罗正鹏
英文审订	【美】Andrew Bauer
英文编辑	辛　颖
版式设计	北京彩奇风企业管理策划有限公司
责任印制	邝　天
出版发行	北京语言大学出版社
社　　址	北京市海淀区学院路15号　邮政编码:100083
网　　址	www.blcup.com
电　　话	编辑部 8610-8230 1016
	发行部 8610-8230 3650/3591/3648
	读者服务部 8610-8230 3653/3908
网上订购	8610-8230 3668（国内）　service@blcup.com
印　　刷	天津嘉恒印务有限公司
经　　销	全国新华书店
版　　次	2014年6月第1版　2022年10月第5次印刷
开　　本	787mm×1092mm　1/16　印张：9.25
字　　数	197千字
书　　号	ISBN 978-7-5619-3679-5 / H·13267
定　　价	88.00元

凡有印装质量问题，本社负责调换。电话：8610-8230 3590

Printed in China

前　言

《中国文化欣赏读本》与《中国文化欣赏》DVD 配套，力图从多个角度生动鲜活地展示中国丰富多彩的文化。本书既可以作为面向中外各界人士的读物，也可以作为汉语学习者的教材。

在内容上，本书选取的文化主题来源于美国汉语教学第一线，是在密歇根州立大学孔子学院的调研结果的基础上确定的，既涵盖了当地汉语教材中的文化点，也尽可能地照顾到了外国人对中国文化的兴趣点。

在编排上，本书每一个文化主题由四个小板块组成，即"导入"、"正文"、"三言两语"、"小链接"。"导入"试图通过各种人物、事件或场景使读者轻松愉快地进入主题，"正文"是对每一主题较为全面、深入的介绍，"三言两语"是中外各界人士对相应主题的评价或感受，"小链接"旨在拓展与主题相关的知识面。需要说明的是，为了让读者看到一些真实材料，我们没有修改"三言两语"中外国朋友们汉语说得不太准确的地方。

本书图文并茂，尽可能使中国文化直观可感，且全书所有内容均为中英文对照，使读者可以通过双语来很好地理解所有内容。

《中国文化欣赏读本》既可与《中国文化欣赏》DVD 配套使用，也可单独使用，因为本书与 DVD 虽然所选主题相同，但都自成体系，二者之间既有内在的联系，分开使用也不影响各自的完整性。作为编者，我们真诚地希望本书能对外国朋友理解与欣赏中国文化有所裨益。

编者

2014 年 1 月

FOREWORD

Exploring Chinese Culture, A Chinese Reader is a supplementary book to the DVD version of *Exploring Chinese Culture*. This book, a vivid presentation of the rich and colorful Chinese culture, can not only be used as reading material for domestic and foreign readers of different walks of life, but can also serve as a textbook for learners of Chinese.

The cultural themes in this book are selected from the forefront of Chinese teaching in America following the survey conducted by the Confucius Institute at Michigan State University. It not only contains the cultural elements of Chinese textbooks in Michigan, but also fully considers foreigner interest regarding Chinese culture.

The cultural themes in this book comprise four sections, "Introduction", "Text", "A Few Remarks" and "Additional Information". The "Introduction" section initiates readers into the topic by presenting various characters, events or backgrounds; the "Text" is a comprehensive and in-depth description of the theme; "A Few Remarks" contains the comments or feedback provided by people from different walks of life, both in China and abroad; "Additional Information" is designed as an extension of knowledge related to the theme. It should be noted that, we didn't revise the non-native Chinese produced by some foreigners so as to present readers with real language materials.

The articles are accompanied by excellent illustrations helpful for a direct and vivid experience of Chinese culture. In addition, the bilingual (English and Chinese) contents of this book assist for a more rapid and better understanding of the cultural themes.

Exploring Chinese Culture, A Chinese Reader can either be used together with the DVD version of *Exploring Chinese Culture*, or used independently. Though the book has the same cultural themes with the DVD, they in fact possess independent systems, thus can be used separately without losing their completeness. As the compilers of this book, we sincerely hope it can prove beneficial to foreigner understanding of Chinese culture.

The Compilers

January, 2014

目录

CONTENTS

◎ 传统节日　Traditional Festivals

002　清明节　|　The Qingming Festival

008　端午节　|　The Duanwu Festival

013　重阳节　|　The Chongyang Festival

◎ 中国艺术　Chinese Arts

020　国画　|　Traditional Chinese Painting

025　书法　|　Chinese Calligraphy

031　印章　|　Chinese Seal

◎ 生活在中国　Living in China

036　胡同与四合院　|　Hutong and Siheyuan

041　玩偶　|　Dolls

046　筷子　|　Chopsticks

051　问候礼节　|　Greeting Etiquette

056　小学生的一天　|　One Day of Elementary Students

◎ 文化符号　Chinese Culture Symbols

062　印刷术　|　Printing

067　灯笼　|　Lantern

名胜古迹　Tourism Highlights

074　长城 ｜ The Great Wall

080　故宫 ｜ The Imperial Palace

085　乐山大佛 ｜ The Leshan Giant Buddha

民间工艺　Folk Arts

092　中国结 ｜ Chinese Knot

097　皮影 ｜ Shadow Play

102　刺绣 ｜ Chinese Embroidery

108　面塑 ｜ Dough Modeling

113　年画 ｜ New Year Picture

民间运动　Folk Sports

120　毽子 ｜ Shuttlecock

125　风筝 ｜ Chinese Kite

130　武术—器械术 ｜ Martial Arts–Weapon Wielding

136　秧歌 ｜ Yangge

Traditional Festivals

传统节日

清明节
The Qingming Festival

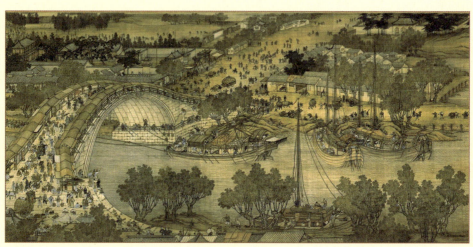

[宋] 张择端《清明上河图》（北京故宫博物院藏）
[Northern Song Dynasty] Riverside Scene at the Qingming Festival by Zhang Zeduan (reserved in The Palace Museum)

在2010年上海世界博览会上，中国馆的镇馆之宝是巨型动态版的《清明上河图》，其恢宏的场面令人震惊。《清明上河图》是北宋（960—1127）画家张择端创作的城市风俗长卷，描绘了清明时节北宋都城汴梁的繁华景象及汴河两岸的自然风光。人物画得尤其生动，有挑担的、骑马的、坐轿的，看上去好像刚刚从郊外踏青、扫墓归来。

In the Expo 2010 Shanghai China, the top treasure of the China Pavilion was the large and dynamic *Riverside Scene at the Qingming Festival* of shocking magnificence. Painted by Zhang Zeduan in the Northern Song Dynasty (960-1127), the *Riverside Scene at Qingming Festival*, a long picture scroll about city customs, describes the bustling scene of Bianliang, the capital city of the Northern Song, and the natural landscape on the banks of Bianhe River during the Qingming Festival. The people in the picture are vividly painted. Some are carrying a load, some are riding a horse, and some others are sitting on a sedan. They all seem to have just had an outing or had just swept the tombs.

"清明"是中国二十四节气之一，也是一个重要的传统节日，一般在四月五日前后。汉语中有不少关于"清明"的谚语，如"清明前后，种瓜点豆"，反映了"清明"作为节气与农业生产的密切关系。作为节日，"清明"又包含着一些特殊的风俗与文化内涵，其名称的来源更是富有诗意："春分后十五日，斗指丁，为清明，时万物皆洁齐而清明，盖时当气清景明，万物皆显，因此得名。"①

As one of the 24 solar terms in China as well as an important traditional festival, Qingming (pure brightness) usually falls around the 5th of April. Many proverbs in Chinese are related to the Qingming Festival such as "to grow melons and beans around the Qingming Festival!" which reflects the close relationship between the solar term Qingming and agricultural production. As a festival, Qingming has some special customs and cultural connotations. It derives its name in a very poetic way. "Fifteen days after the Spring Equinox, the Big Dipper points to *Ding* (the fourth hour at night in the ancient subdivision system of a day) in the sky and thus Qingming begins. At that time, everything is clean, delicate and pretty. Perhaps Qingming is called so because everything comes back to life in the clean and bright atmosphere seen during that time."①

清明时节颐和园的美景，田琨摄
The beautiful scene of the Summer Palace during the Qingming Festival, photographed by Tian Kun

唐代以前，清明节前一天（一说清明节前两天）叫"寒食节"，这一天不能生火煮饭，家家都要吃冷食。寒食节是由古代禁旧火、换新火的制度演变而来的。古时候人们钻木取火，所钻树木的种类因季节的不同而变化，因此每到春天换取新火便成为

Before the Tang Dynasty, the day before the Qingming Festival (or one or two days before the Qingming Festival) is called the Cold Food Festival when people can eat nothing but cold food instead of making fire or cooking. The Cold Food Festival evolves from the ancient rule of forbidding the old fire and changing into the new fire. Changing to new fire every spring is quite important because the wood used by ancient people varies in different seasons. Since making fire is forbidden before getting

---

①语出《历书》，该书是中国历史上著名的天文学著作，隋代天文学家刘焯所作。

① From *Almanac*, a famous astronomical book in Chinese history written by Liu Zhuo, an astronomer in the Sui Dynasty.

一件大事。在新火没取到的时候是禁止生火的，于是人们就准备了一些冷食以备食用。唐代（618—907）以后，"寒食"与"清明"合二为一，"清明"成为一个固定的节日，流传至今的习俗主要有扫墓、踏青、荡秋千和放风筝等。

扫墓又叫"祭墓"，是中国人祭奠祖先和已故亲人的一种方式。除了祭祀家族的祖先外，清明节也要祭祀中华民族共同的祖先，这一习俗反映了传统农业社会和儒家文化对中国节日文化的影响。

踏青又叫"春游"。清明时节大地回春，自然界到处呈现出生机勃勃的景象，草长莺飞，桃红柳绿，正是外出郊游的好时光。由于踏青是一项非常有益于身心的活动，因此自古以来一直深受人们喜爱。

the new fire, people prepare some cold food to eat. After the Tang Dynasty (618-907), the Cold Food Festival and Qingming Festival were combined into one and the Qingming Festival became a fixed festival. Some customs still remain today such as the sweeping of the tomb, having an outing in spring, playing on swings and flying kites.

Sweeping the tomb, also called offering sacrifices to the tomb, serves as a way for Chinese people to offer sacrifices to ancestors and the dead relatives. During the Qingming Festival, people will offer sacrifices not only to the ancestors of their own families but also to the common ancestor of the Chinese nation, a custom that reflects the influence of traditional agricultural society and Confucian culture on Chinese festival culture traditions.

Having an outing in spring is called *taqing* or *chunyou* in Chinese. The Qingming Festival is a good time for outings because the spring returns

踏青，田琨摄
Having an outing in spring, photographed by Tian Kun

荡秋千源自古代北方少数民族的习武活动，宋代（960—1279）以后，荡秋千的活动从宫廷普及到民间。相传儿童做秋千之戏可以去百病，因而在中国不少地区都有清明荡

to the earth at that time and the nature is full of vigor with growing grasses, flying nightingales, red peach blossoms and green willows. Having an outing has been quite popular among people since ancient times for being good for both physical and mental health.

荡秋千
Playing on the swing

秋千的习俗。

放风筝源自古代的巫术。古人认为，放飞的风筝可以带走疾病与厄运。清明节时放风筝不仅是一种娱乐活动，而且有利于身体健康。据说世界上第一个风筝是春秋时代著名的工匠鲁班用木头制作的。东汉（25—220）以后出现

Playing on swings originated from the martial art practice of ancient northern minorities. After the Song Dynasty (960-1279), this custom spread from the palace into the folk. It is said that children can rid themselves of all diseases by playing on swings. Therefore, the custom of playing on swings during the Qingming Festival still remains in some regions in China.

Flying kites stemmed from ancient sorcery. Ancient people believe that flying kites can take away disease and misfortune. Flying kites during the Qingming Festival were not only entertaining but also conducive to good health. It is said that the first kite was made of wood by the famous craftsman Lu Ban in the Spring and Autumn Period. In the Eastern Han Dynasty (25-220), the first paper-made kite appeared with the name *zhiyuan* (paper eagle). Late, after a bamboo flute was added to the head of *zhiyuan*,

放风筝　*Flying the kite*

了纸做的风筝，叫"纸鸢"，后来有人在纸鸢的头上加了一个竹笛，纸鸢飞上天后被风一吹便发出"呜呜"的声音，好像筝的弹奏声，于是人们就给纸鸢改了名称，叫"风筝"。在中国，风筝的制作有三大流派，北京、天津和山东潍坊的风筝都很有特色，享誉中外。

zhiyuan had its name changed into fengzheng (wind zheng) because of it, when flying into the sky and being blown by the wind, sounds like the whine of zheng, a kind of Chinese zither. In China, the three schools of kites—the kites in Beijing, Tianjin and Weifang of Shandong Province—enjoy high reputation all around the world due to their distinguished features.

三言两语 A FEW REMARKS

清明节的主题，一是认祖归宗、怀念亲人，二是对大自然的亲和。不少人把清明节等节日当成普通的假日对待，缺乏对节日内容的记忆与情感释放，这对节日文化传承非常不利。若想促使全民对节日实现集体认同，就必须从孩子抓起，让孩子们在节日中享受中华文化，这是我们的责任。

[中国] 冯骥才，男，作家

在我的老家甘肃，清明节那天上午要去祭扫祖坟，有的地方只有男的才能去扫墓，女的是不能去的。此外，清明节还要拿一些艾草插在房门上，有辟邪的意思，还有清扫不干净东西的作用。

[中国] 林森，男，工人

我觉得中国的清明节和我们国家的盂兰盆节差不多。每年阴历七月十五，我们会放七天假，大家利用假期返回故乡，祭祖扫墓，探亲访友。这一天交通很繁忙，有点儿像中国的"春运"，有人叫它"民族大移动"。

[日本] 山田百合，女，大学生

The themes of the Qingming Festival are to return home and miss the relatives and to get close to nature. Quite a few people treat the Qingming Festival as nothing but an ordinary holiday without the memory or emotions of the festival, which is quite harmful for the inheritance of the festival culture. In order to realize the whole nation's recognition of this festival, we must start from the children and take responsibility as to let children enjoy Chinese culture in the festival.

[China] Feng Jicai, male, writer

During the Qingming Festival in my native place of Gansu Province, we will sweep the tombs of our ancestors. In some regions, only males are allowed to sweep the tomb. Moreover, we will also put the argy wormwood on the door to counteract evil forces and also to clean up dirty things.

[China] Lin Sen, male, worker

I think that the Qingming Festival in China is quite similar to our Obon Festival. We have seven days off around every July 15th in the lunar calendar. At that time, we will go back home to sweep the tombs of our ancestors and visit friends and relatives. The traffic is quite busy during those days and similar to the Spring Festival Travel in China. Therefore, some people call it "a Big Move of the Whole Nation".

[Japan] Yamada Yuri, female, university student

潍坊风筝
Kites in Weifang

　　山东潍坊是中国的风筝之乡，风筝制作不仅历史悠久，而且样式精美，题材多样，具有浓郁的生活气息。潍坊国际风筝节是中国最有名的风筝盛会，自1984年举办第一届以来，每年在清明之后的4月20 — 25日都要举办一次。1988年潍坊荣获"世界风筝之都"的美誉，1989年"国际风筝联合会"决定把总部设在潍坊，从此潍坊成为世界风筝文化交流的中心。

Weifang in Shandong Province is home to kites in China. With a long history of production, the kites have elegant styles, various themes, and a rich flavor of life. The Weifeng International Kite Festival, the most well-known kite festival in China, is held from April 20th to April 25th after the Qingming Festival every year since it began in 1984. Weifang was reputed as the "capital of kites in the world" in 1988 and selected as headquarters of the International Kite Federation in 1989. From then on, Weifang has become the center of international communication regarding kite culture.

端午节
The Duanwu Festival

"粽子香，香厨房。艾叶香，香满堂。桃枝插在大门上，出门一望麦儿黄。这儿端阳，那儿端阳。处处都端阳。"这是一首描写端午习俗的民谣。端午节又称"端阳节"，日期在农历五月初五。从节日活动来看，端午节习俗的主要目的是预防疾病与促进人际交往。

端午节的粽子
Rice dumplings in the Duanwu Festival

"The enticing smell of the rice dumplings and the mugwort leaves fills the kitchen and even the whole house. The peach twig is put on the door and the wheat is yellow outside the door. The Duanwu Festival has arrived. The Duanwu Festival is here and there and everywhere." This is a folk song describing the customs of the Duanwu Festival. The Duanwu Festival is also called Duanyang Festival in Chinese and falls on May 5th in the lunar calendar. From the perspective of festival activities, the main customs of the festival are mainly to prevent diseases and promote interpersonal communication.

在中国，端午节是一个集驱瘟辟邪、游戏竞技、饮食娱乐与社交往来为一体的重要节日，端午节的传统习俗很多，主要有赛龙舟、吃粽子、挂菖蒲、插艾草、饮药酒、系五色丝线、贴五毒图案等。

赛龙舟又叫"龙舟竞渡"，是端午节最盛大的活动。龙舟是一种装饰成龙形的船，这和中国人对龙的信

In China, the Duanwu Festival is an important festival combining casting away diseases and evil spirits, playing games and sports, and interpersonal communication. Among the many customs of the festival mainly are dragon-boat racing, eating of rice dumplings, hanging of calamus and wormwood, drinking of medical liquor, tying silk threads of five colors, and pasting pictures portraying the five poisonous creatures.

仰有关。据闻一多先生研究，端午节原来是祭祀龙的节日。远古时代，南方的吴越民族由于不断受到水旱灾害的威胁，就把龙作为本民族的祖先和保护神，每到农历五月都要举行盛大的图腾祭祀活动：人们将装在竹筒中或裹在树叶里的食物扔到水中献给图腾神吃；为了让神高兴还要在急鼓声中划着龙舟在水上竞渡。由于历史和文化传统的差异，中国各地的龙舟在样式、比赛方式与规模等方面都有所不同，甚至具体日期也不太一样。作为一项体育竞技项目，龙舟竞赛还传播到东亚和东南亚的一些国家，如日本、韩国、越南、泰国等。随着社会的进步与男女平等意识的增强，过去不允许妇女参加的龙舟竞渡活动如今也吸引了不少英姿飒爽的女性，她们

赛龙舟　*Dragon-boat racing*

为端午节的竞渡活动增添了一道亮丽的色彩。

　　关于端午节吃粽子的来源，中国民间广泛流传的说法是为了纪念战国时期（前475—前221）楚国伟大的

Dragon-boat racing is the biggest event of the Duanwu Festival. The dragon boat is a boat decorated in the shape of dragon because of Chinese people's belief in dragons. According to the research of Wen Yiduo, the Duanwu Festival used to be a festival to offer sacrifices to dragons. In ancient times, the Wuyue nation in South China would hold a grand ceremony to worship the totem in the fifth lunar month every year because they were constantly threatened by floods and droughts and regarded the dragon as their ancestor and patron. People would put the food in the bamboo tube or leaves into the water so that the totem god could eat it. In order to delight the god, people also raced dragon boats in the river amid the rushing beating of drums. As a result of the differences in history and cultural tradition, places around China now differ from each other in boat style, race mode and scale and even race date. As a kind of sport, dragon-boat racing even spread to some countries in East Asia and Southeast Asia such as Japan, South Korea, Vietnam and Thailand. Due to social progress and growing awareness of gender equality, some valiant and heroic women are also attracted by the dragon-boat racing which they were not allowed to participate in during the past, and this makes the race much more colorful.

爱国主义诗人屈原。他热爱自己的国家，敢于在国君面前讲真话，但由于小人陷害被流放到很远的地方。当他听到楚国的国都被秦国攻占以后，悲愤地投了汨罗江。人们非常怀念他，便用竹筒盛上米投入江中，此习俗后来演变为包粽子。

汉白玉雕屈原像
Qu Yuan's sculpture in white marble

挂菖蒲、插艾草、饮药酒、系五色丝线、贴五毒图案等也是端午节的传统习俗。菖蒲、艾草用来辟邪，药酒用来保健，五色丝线与五毒图案都是为保安康的。五色丝线不可任意折断或丢弃，只能在夏季大雨中或洗澡时抛到河里，意味着让河水将瘟疫、

In regard to the origin of eating rice dumplings in the Duanwu Festival, the widespread belief among people is that it is to commemorate Qu Yuan, a great patriotic poet of the Chu State during the Warring States Period (475-221 BC). Qu Yuan dared to tell the truth before the monarch out of love for his own country but got exiled to a distant place after being framed by some others. When it came to him that the capital of the Chu State was occupied by the Qin State, he was so grieved and indignant that he drowned himself into the Miluo River. After that, people missed him very much and put rice in bamboo tubes and threw them into the river. Later, this custom was transformed into the making of rice dumplings.

Hanging calamus and wormwood, drinking medical liquor, tying silk threads of five colors, and pasting pictures of the five poisonous creatures are also customs of the Duanwu Festival. Calamus and wormwood are used to exorcise evil spirits; medical liquor is used for health care; silk threads of five colors and pictures of the five poisonous creatures are both used to ensure security and good health. The silk threads of five colors cannot be broken voff or discarded but should be thrown into the river in the summer rain or while bathing, meaning that the river will wash away plagues and diseases. The five poisonous creatures refer to scorpions, vipers, centipedes, house lizards and toads. In the era with underdeveloped science and culture, pasting pictures of the five poisonous creatures aimed at removing ill fortune and praying for good fortune. With the development of modern civilization, these

疾病冲走；五毒是指蛇、蝎子、壁虎、蜈蚣、蟾蜍五种有毒的害虫，在科学文化不发达的时代，贴五毒图意在祛毒禳灾、求福纳吉。随着现代社会文明的发展，这些古老的习俗日益淡化，而饮食、娱乐和社交等功能更加突出。

五毒耳枕
Children's pillow with the images of the five poisonous creatures on it

old customs gradually faded and the festival became an opportunity for eating, entertaining and social intercourse more than ever before.

三言两语 A FEW REMARKS

我记得小时候，端午节还没到，家里就准备包粽子，采摘苇叶，购买馅料。过端午节时门上要插艾草，大家在一起吃粽子、鸭蛋、绿豆糕。我们还会把煮熟的鸭蛋带到学校去，和小伙伴对对碰，看谁的鸭蛋结实……现在好像吃吃粽子就算过节了。

[中国] 李蕾，女，公司职员

其实除了吃，粽子还代表了一种礼节。北京的粽子类似心形，粽子虽小却可表感恩之心，凡是对自己有过恩惠的人，到端午这一天要给他送粽子。过去老北京人都讲究在自己家里包粽子，用粽子当礼品送给邻居。原来粽子的包装没有现在这么精美，大大小小的粽子用线串在一起，名为"九连粽"，送人的时候更显心意和祝福的诚挚。

[中国] 赵书，男，民俗专家

I remember that when I was young, my family members began to prepare for making rice dumplings before the Duanwu Festival. They would pick the reed leaves and buy fillings. During the festival, people would place the wormwood on the door and eat rice dumplings, duck eggs and green bean cakes together. We would also take the cooked duck eggs to school to test which egg is more uneasily broken by knocking the eggs against those of our little friends. Nowadays, however, it seems that people celebrate the festival just by eating rice dumplings.

[China] Li Lei, female, company employee

In fact, rice dumplings were not only served as a type of food but also to represent a kind of formality. The heart-shaped rice dumplings in Beijing, despite their small sizes, are symbolic of gratitude. People will give rice dumplings to those who have helped them during the Duanwu Festival. In the past, people in Beijing always made rice dumplings at home and gave them to their neighbors as gifts. At that time, the rice dumplings were not as delicately packed as those in these days. Rice dumplings of different sizes were strung together with threads and called *jiulianzong* (nine rice dumplings together) which is more capable to demonstrate the kindly feelings and express the sincere wishes.

[China] Zhao Shu, male, folklorist

我觉得这不是澳洲人的看法，是我自己的。我第一次体会端午节是我去台湾旅行的时候，那时我什么中国节都不知道。我到女朋友的家乡以后，她说因为端午节快到了，所以人比较多。她也给我简单地解释了端午节是怎么产生的，还有吃粽子和划龙舟的含义。我没看过龙舟比赛，可我吃过好多粽子。中国历史很长，也很有意思，所以我喜欢，中国有很多跟澳洲完全不同的地方，所以给我不一样的感觉。

[澳大利亚] 何克帆，男，大学生

I think this is my own opinion but not all Australians. I experienced the Duanwu Festival for the first time when I travelled in Taiwan and knew nothing about China. After arriving at my girlfriend's home, I was told that there were many people there because the Duanwu Festival was coming. My girlfriend also briefly explained to me the origin of the festival as well as the meaning of eating rice dumplings and rowing dragon boats. I didn't watch the dragon-boat race but ate a lot of rice dumplings. I love the long and interesting Chinese history. Many things in China are totally different from those in Australia and they give me different feelings.

[Australia] He Kefan, male, university student

小链接 ADDITIONAL INFORMATION

苗族龙船节
The Dragon-boat Festival of the Miao nationality

除汉族以外，中国一些少数民族也有在农历五月吃粽子、赛龙舟的习俗。例如居住在贵州省东南部的苗族每年农历五月二十四日至二十七日，都要在清水江边举行盛大的"龙船节"。当地的龙舟与常见的不同，由三只独木舟联成"子母船"，中间较长的一只称"母船"，船上有鼓手指挥，两边的船稍短，称"子船"。比赛时，河岸两边站满了前来观看的人们，擂鼓声与呐喊助威声不断，场面十分热闹、壮观。

Apart from the Han nationality, some ethnic groups in China also have the customs of eating rice dumplings and rowing dragon boats in the fifth lunar month. For instance, the Miao nationality in the southeast of Guizhou Province holds the grand Dragon-boat Festival by the Qingshui River every year from May 24th to May 27th of the lunar calendar. The local dragon boats are different from the commonly seen ones. The Child-Mother boat is made of three canoes. The long canoe in the middle is called Mother Boat controlled by drummers on it while the two short canoes on the two sides are called Child Boats. During the race, both banks of the river are crowded with people who come to watch the race amid the constant beating of drums and the sounds of cheering and shouting, thus creating a lively and magnificent scene.

重阳节
The Chongyang Festival

导入
INTRODUCTION

"独在异乡为异客，每逢佳节倍思亲。遥知兄弟登高处，遍插茱萸少一人。"这首脍炙人口的诗是唐代诗人王维创作的《九月九日忆山东兄弟》，诗中描写了唐代重阳登高的习俗，表达了作者思念家乡和亲人的情感。

"All alone in a foreign land, I am twice as home sick on this day. When brothers carry dogwood up the mountain, each of them a branch—and my branch missing." The popular poem "Thinking of My Brothers In Shandong On Mountain Climbing Day" written by the poet Wang Wei in the Tang Dynasty describes the custom of climbing mountains in the Chongyang Festival (Double Ninth Festival)and expresses the feelings of missing the hometown and the family.

云台山的王维雕像，田琨摄
The sculpture of Wang Wei in Yuntai Mountain, photographed by Tian Kun

重阳节在农历九月初九，中国古代以一、三、五、七、九为阳数，以二、四、六、八、十为阴数。因为"九"与"九"两阳相重，所以九月九日叫"重阳"，又叫"重九"。

重阳节历史悠久，一般认为在春秋战国时期就已受到人们重视，不过当时还只是在宫廷中进行庆祝。到西汉（前206—公元25）时逐渐由宫

The Chongyang Festival falls on September 9th of the lunar calendar and is also called the Chongjiu Festival. Ancient Chinese regard one, three, five, seven and nine as *yang* numbers and two, four, six, eight, and ten as *yin* numbers. The lunar September 9th is called *chong yang* (double *yang*) or *chong jiu* (double nine) because it has two *yang* "nines".

It is generally thought that the Chongyang Festival, with a long history, has received

廷传入民间。重阳节的习俗主要有登高、赏菊、戴茱萸、吃重阳花糕等。

重阳节登高的习俗与季节有密切的关系。农历九月正值金秋，菊花盛开，丹桂飘香，天气晴朗，风光旖旎，此时正是去郊外野游和爬山的大好时节。重阳登高的活动在唐代（618—907）特别流行，每到重阳节时，无论男女老少都要到郊外登高，目的是为了强身健体，延年益寿。

登高远望——无限风光在险峰，田琨摄
Ascending a height to enjoy a distant view—infinite beauty in the perilous peak, photographed by Tian Kun

古代人们在过重阳节时还要佩戴茱萸，茱萸是一种具有浓烈香味的植物，可以做中药，并有驱蚊杀虫的作用。古时人们认为把这种植物戴在头上可以辟除恶气，抵御秋末冬初的寒气，保平安，保健康。

people's attention since the Spring and Autumn Period and the Warring States Period but was only celebrated in the palace at that time. It was spread among the common people in the Western Han Dynasty (206 BC-AD 25). The customs of the Chongyang Festival mainly include climbing mountains, appreciating chrysanthemums, wearing dogwoods and eating Chongyang cakes.

The custom of climbing mountains during the Chongyang Festival is closely associated with the season. Lunar September, with blooming chrysanthemums, strong fragrances of laurel blossoms, clear autumn weather and beautiful scenery, is a good time for an outing in the suburbs and climbing mountains. In the Tang Dynasty (618-907), climbing mountains during the Chongyang Festival was so popular that people of all ages and both sexes climbed mountains in the countryside with the purpose of building body and prolonging life.

Ancient people also wore dogwoods during the Chongyang Festival. Dogwood, as a plant with strong fragrance, can be used as a kind of Chinese medicine and also as something to repel mosquitoes and kill insects. In ancient times, people believe that wearing dogwood

重阳花糕
Chongyang cake

花糕是重阳节的传统食品，用米粉、豆粉、果料等原料制成。自唐、宋（960—1279）以后，重阳节吃花糕成为一种时尚，有些地方还把花糕制成九层，像一座小山。因为"糕"与"高"谐音，吃花糕即象征"步步登高"。

赏菊和饮菊花酒也是重阳节的主要习俗。古时人们就认为菊花有清热明目等作用，长期饮用菊花酒可以延年益寿，所以，菊花酒被中国民间认为是最实用的药酒。中国人不仅爱饮菊花酒，而且喜爱赏菊，这主要是因为人们赞赏菊花的品格。因为农历九月，已近晚秋，草木枯黄，而菊花却"芬然独秀"，因此，古人把农历九月称为"菊月"，以表示对菊花临霜不凋的赞美。在中国古代文人中，晋代（265—420）诗人陶渊明（约365—427）是最爱菊花的，他写的菊花诗也很有名。到清代（1616—1911）时，有的地方还要在重阳节期间举办盛大的菊花宴、菊花会，这种习俗一直延

on their heads would make it possible to keep away evil spirits, resist chillness at the end of autumn and the beginning of winter, and ensure security and good health.

The Chongyang cake, a traditional food of the festival, is made of rice flour, bean flour and fruit materials. After the Tang and the Song dynasties (960-1279), eating Chongyang cakes in the Chongyang Festival became fashionable. People in some places make cakes of nine layers like a small hill. Since cake in Chinese is pronounced as "gao", which is the same with the pronunciation of "高" (height) in Chinese, eating Chongyang cakes symbolizes getting higher step by step.

Appreciating chrysanthemums and drinking chrysanthemum wine are also important customs of the Chongyang Festival. Since ancient times, people have regarded chrysanthemum wine as the most effective medical liquor because they believe that chrysanthemum can clear away heat and improve eyesight and that longtime drinking of chrysanthemum wine is able to prolong life. Chinese people love not only to drink chrysanthemum wine but also to appreciate chrysanthemums mainly out of their admiration of the character of chrysanthemums. On September 9th of the lunar calendar, grass and leaves are withered and yellow in the late autumn while chrysanthemums are still in bloom and give out fragrance. Therefore, ancient Chinese call lunar September "the month of the chrysanthemum" to express their admiration of chrysanthemums which do not wither away in frost. Among ancient Chinese scholars, Tao Yuanming (about 365-427) in the Jin Dynasty

北京植物园的菊花节，田琨摄
Chrysanthemum Festival in the Beijing Botanical Garden, photographed by Tian Kun

(265-420) loved chrysanthemums most and wrote many famous poems about chrysanthemums. In the Qing Dynasty (1616-1911), grand chrysanthemum feasts and shows were held in some regions during the Chongyang Festival, a custom that remains alive today. Around the Chongyang Festival, chrysanthemum shows are held all around China and people also visit gardens to appreciate chrysanthemums.

续到今天。在重阳节前后，中国各地都要举办菊花展和游园赏菊活动。

　　1989年，中国政府把农历九月九日定为"老人节"，又称"敬老节"，因为"九"与"久"谐音，象征长寿。在这一天，不少机关、团体、社区都会组织退休老人秋游或参加登山活动，以强身健体，愉悦身心；在不少家庭中，晚辈也会特地为老人准备一些可口的饮食。尊老、敬老是中华民族的优良传统，这种风尚在重阳节中也得到了充分体现。

In 1989, the Chinese government designated lunar September 9th as the Seniors' Day, which is also regarded as the Day for Respecting the Aged because the pronunciation of nine in Chinese is the same with that of "久" ("jiu", longevity) and thus nine is symbolic of long life. On that day, many institutions, groups and communities organize retired seniors for an outing in autumn or mountain climbing in order to build their bodies while having fun. In many families, younger people will specially prepare some delicious food for the seniors. The fine tradition of respecting the elderly of the Chinese nation is fully demonstrated in the Chongyang Festival.

三言两语 A FEW REMARKS

　　我从上大学就开始离开家，除了春节几乎所有的节日包括父母的生日都没有在一起过过，每到过属于他们的节日时，心里多少有些歉意，也有许多不忍心。一转眼就七八年了，只能靠电话传送祝福及关心。在重阳节，这个老人节只能祝福父母平安健康，幸福开心。

　　[中国] 方慧慧，女，幼儿教师

I left home after attending university and cannot celebrate festivals with my parents except for the Spring Festival. I even have not celebrated their birthdays since then. Therefore, I feel sorry and regretful more or less during the festivals. In the past seven or eight years which have passed so quickly, I can only express my wishes and care through the phone. In the Chongyang Festival, a festival of the elderly, I can only wish my parents safety, health and happiness.

[China] Fang Huihui, female, kindergarten teacher

　　我对重阳节印象比较深，小时候，经常听父母说重阳节到了，螃蟹肥了，菊花黄了。每到重阳节都能吃到好吃的重阳糕，还有螃蟹。因此，我对重阳节还是有期盼的。

　　[中国] 陈玉峰，男，个体户

I have a deep impression of the Chongyang Festival. When I was a child, I often heard from my parents that the Chongyang Festival came and that the crabs got fat and the chrysanthemums turned yellow. I could eat delicious Chongyang cakes and crabs during every Chongyang Festival. Therefore, I looked forward to this festival.
[China] Chen Yufeng, male, self-employed businessman

　　重阳节是中国的老人节，我们的老人节是笑节，在每年的6月21日。这一天，书店里会展出幽默类图书，喜剧演员会表演滑稽节目，电视台也专门推出一台晚会，招待老人，引起老人大笑。我们相信笑能促进老人健康长寿。

　　[加拿大] 艾奥纳，女，留学生

The Seniors' Day is the Chongyang Festival in China but the Seniors' Day in our country is the Smiling Festival which falls on June 21st every year. On that day, bookshops exhibit humorous books and comedians give funny performances. TV stations also broadcast evening parties to entertain the elderly and provoke their laughter. We believe that laughter contributes to seniors' good health and long life.
[Canada] Iona, female, foreign student

小链接 ADDITIONAL INFORMATION

月光下的红叶，田琨摄
Red leaves in the moonlight, photographed by Tian Kun

　　唐代诗人杜牧（803—约852）曾在《山行》中写道："远上寒山石径斜，白云深处有人家。停车坐爱枫林晚，霜叶红于二月花。"生动描绘了秋天山野层林尽染的景色。北京的香山是清代著名皇家园林，也是重阳登高的好去处，每年10月举办的"香山红叶节"吸引了海内外众多游客前来观赏。

Du Mu (803-about 852), a poet in the Tang Dynasty, wrote in "Tour on a Mountain" that "The stone-paved path zigzags up to the cliff in the distance, households are seen where waft some white clouds. I stop the coach as charmed by the maple woods, frosted autumn leaves outshine February flowers in redness." This poem vividly describes the scenery of mountains and forests all tinged in autumn. The Fragrant Hill in Beijing is a famous royal garden of the Qing Dynasty as well as a good place for mountain climbing in the Chongyang Festival. The Red Leaf Festival in the Fragrant Hill attracts a great many visitors from home and abroad each October.

Chinese Arts

中国艺术

国　画
Traditional Chinese Painting

齐白石画的虾活灵活现
The lifelike shrimps drawn by Qi Baishi

　　齐白石（1864—1957）是中国著名的国画大师，擅画花鸟、虫鱼、山水、人物。齐白石的画笔墨滋润，色彩明快，造型生动，意境幽远，画虾尤为一绝，活灵活现，妙趣横生。

As a well-known master of traditional Chinese painting, Qi Baishi was good at drawing flowers, birds, insects, fish, landscapes, fish, humans, and especially shrimps. The lifelike shrimps drawn by him are quite interesting and entertaining. Never stinting himself in pen and ink, he draws pictures with bright colors, vivid shapes, and deep artistic meanings.

　　"国画"是"中国画"的简称，指用毛笔蘸水、墨、彩，画在绢、纸、帛上的绘画作品，题材可分为人物、山水、花鸟等，技法可分为工笔、写意等。国画以具象的方式体现了中国人对大自然和人类社会的认识。

　　国画的历史十分悠久，可以追溯到新石器时代的岩画和彩陶上的图案，不过保留至今具有独立绘画意义的最早作品是战国时期的两幅帛画《人物龙凤图》和《人物御龙图》，这些早期绘画奠定了后世国画以线条为主要造型手段的基础。

Zhongguohua (traditional Chinese painting), guohua in short, refers to paintings drawn on silk and paper by writing brush in water, ink or color. The subjects include human figures, landscapes, and flowers and birds. The techniques can be divided into fine brushwork, freehand brushwork and so on. The traditional Chinese paintings reflect Chinese people's understanding of nature and human society in a representational way.

With a long history, traditional Chinese painting can be traced back to the cliff painting and pictures on colored pottery in the Neolithic Age. The earliest works with independent significance of paintings that are

新石器时代人面鱼纹盆（中国国家博物馆藏）
Basin painted with the design of human face and fish in the Neolithic Age (reserved in National Museum of China)

　　在漫长的历史发展过程中，国画在不同的时期体现出不同的艺术特征与文化内涵。两汉至南北朝社会发生了由统一到分裂的急剧变化，域外文化与本土文化相互碰撞与融合，绘画以宗教人物画、历史人物画为主，同时出现了画论。隋唐经济发达、文化昌盛，绘画也随之呈现出全面繁荣的局面，人物画达到了顶峰，并出现了世俗化倾向——主要有宗教人物画、政治人物画、仕女画，代表画家有吴道子、阎立本、张萱。除此之外，山水画、花鸟画也十分成熟。五代两宋时期城市获得了大发展，人物画转向描绘世俗生活，宗教画逐渐衰退，山水画、花鸟画跃居画坛主流。元明清时期水墨山水和写意花鸟得到突出发展，文人画和风俗画成为中国画的主流。19世纪末国画引入了西方美术的表现形式与艺术观念，出现了流派纷

reserved up to now are the *Picture of Human, Dragon and Phoenix* and the *Picture of Human Reining the Dragon*, two paintings on silk of the Warring States Period. These early paintings lay the foundation for later people's use of lines as the main modeling method.

In the long history of development, traditional Chinese paintings demonstrate different artistic features and cultural connotations in different periods of time. From the Western Han and Eastern Han dynasties to the Northern and Southern dynasties, the society underwent the rapid change from national unity to disruption. Within the cultural clash and fusion between local culture and foreign culture, most paintings were about religious and historical figures and painting theories also appeared. In the Sui and Tang dynasties with prosperous economy and culture, paintings also entered the period of full bloom. Figure painting reached its peak and tended to be secular. The representative painters were Wu Daozi, Yan Liben and Zhang Xuan. The main types of painting included religious figure painting, political figure painting and beauty painting. Landscape painting and bird-and-flower painting were also quite mature. During the Five Dynasties and the Song dynasty, figure painting focused more on secular life. Religious painting gradually faded while landscape painting and bird-and-flower painting became the mainstream. In the Yuan, Ming and Qing

呈、名家辈出的新局面，如徐悲鸿便将西方绘画的写实手法融入传统的笔墨之中，丰富了中国画的表现性。

[元] 黄公望《水阁清幽图》（南京博物馆藏）
[Yuan Dynasty] Picture of the Quiet and Beautiful Waterside Pavilion by Huang Gongwang (reserved in Nanjing Museum)

与西方的油画相比，中国的国画具有鲜明的特征，例如：国画重线条，用线勾勒出轮廓、质感、体积；油画重色彩，讲究比例、明暗、透视、色度、光感。国画采用散点透视法，即移动立足点进行观察，各个立足点所看到的东西都可组织进自己的画面；油画采用焦点透视法，观察者固定在一个立足点上把看到的东西画下来。国画计白当黑，没有画面的部分也像有画面的部分一样认真处理，

dynasties, ink landscape painting and freehand bird-and-flower painting developed rapidly and painting of man-of-letters and genre painting became the mainstream. At the end of the 19th century when western painting's form of manifestation and artistic conception were introduced into China, there appeared diverse genres and many famous artists. For example, Xu Beihong employed the realistic approach of western paintings in traditional Chinese paintings, thus making them richer and more expressive.

Compared with western oil paintings, traditional Chinese paintings have their distinguished features. For example, traditional Chinese paintings emphasize lines and use lines to create shape, texture and volume while western paintings focus on colors and stress proportion, light and shade, perspective, chroma and light sensation. Traditional Chinese paintings employ the method of cavalier perspective, which means the painter changing the foothold for observation and absorbing everything observed into the painting. Oil paintings, however, use the method of focus perspective, meaning that the observer stands at one point and paints what he or she sees. Traditional Chinese paintings reckon blank space as inked and treat the unpainted space as seriously as the painted space while oil paintings focus on the painted part.

Traditional Chinese paintings are mainly divided into three categories (*hua fen san ke* in Chinese)—figure paintings, flower-and-bird paintings and landscape paintings. In fact, they are categorized based on their artistic

[五代] 顾闳中《韩熙载夜宴图》（北京故宫博物院藏）
[Five Dynasties] Picture of Han Xizai's Evening Banquet by Gu Hongzhong (reserved in Palace Museum)

而油画创作的重点在有画之处。

国画主要有三个种类，即"画分三科"——人物画、花鸟画、山水画。这表面上看是按题材分类的，其实是用艺术表现观念与思想分的类：人物画展示世间万象，表现了人与人之间的关系；山水画将人与自然融为一体，说明人与自然是和谐相处的；花鸟画描绘大自然的各种生命，表现了宇宙中的勃勃生机。凡此种种都是中国艺术的真谛。

expression concepts and thoughts although they seem to be classified according to their subjects. Figure paintings reveal everything in the world as well as interpersonal relationships; landscape paintings combine humans and nature and reveal the harmony between them; flower-and-bird paintings depict all creatures in nature and demonstrate the vigor and vitality of the universe. All of them reveal the essence of Chinese art.

三言两语 A FEW REMARKS

与国画相比，我更喜欢西洋画。我总觉得国画色彩没有那么鲜明，不像西洋画那样充分运用各种色彩，而且画面很饱满，整幅作品没有一处空白，所有的色彩扑面而来，特别有张力。不过，国画注重细节，多一笔嫌多，少一笔不成画，这也是西洋画所比不了的。

[中国] 孙浩淼，男，自由职业者

作为一个从小熟悉油画的外国人，对中国的国画确实很陌生。大部

Compared with traditional Chinese paintings, I prefer western paintings because traditional Chinese paintings do not have vivid colors while western paintings make full use of various colors and leave no blank space in the whole full painting. All colors leap to the eyes and create the effect of tension. However, traditional Chinese paintings stress details and cannot bear one more or one less brushstroke, which cannot be equaled by western paintings.

[China] Sun Haomiao, male, freelancer

Since I am a foreigner familiar with oil paintings since an early age, traditional Chinese paintings are really strange to me. Most Chinese paintings

分都是高山与流水，还有鸡、虫、鸟、蔬菜等等，而且画是一片黑白灰，几乎看不到颜色。这跟西方的油画有巨大的差别。但一开始深刻研究国画就可以发现它的魅力，和它如何反映中国人的审美观。所以外国人要想了解中国古老的文化必须要了解中国的国画。

[奥地利] 齐傲莲，女，大学生

are about high mountains, flowing rivers, chickens, insects, birds and vegetables in black, white or gray without any bright colors, which are greatly different from western oil paintings. However, a profound study of Chinese paintings will help you find their charm and how they reflect Chinese people's aesthetic standard. Therefore, foreigners have to know traditional Chinese paintings in order to understand old Chinese culture.

[Austria] Qi Aolian, female, university student

小链接 ADDITIONAL INFORMATION

油画是西洋画的主要画种，以快干性的植物油如亚麻仁油、罂粟油、核桃油等调和颜料，在亚麻布、纸板或木板上进行创作。画面所附着的颜料有较强的硬度，画面干燥后能长期保持光泽。17世纪是欧洲古典油画迅速发展的时期，不同国家画家的作品体现出不同的社会背景和民族风格。油画的种类按题材可分为历史画、宗教画、肖像画、风景画、静物画、风俗画等。

波提切利《维纳斯的诞生》（意大利佛罗伦萨乌斐齐美术馆藏）
The Birth Of Venus by Botticelli (reserved in the Uffizi Gallery in Florence, Italy)

As the main type of western paintings, oil paintings painted on linen, paperboard and wood board employ fast-drying vegetable oil such as linseed oil, poppy seed oil, and walnut oil to mix the pigments. The pigment on the paintings is characterized by a high degree of hardness so that the colors can be maintained for a long time after the paintings dry. The 17th century witnessed the rapid development of European classical oil paintings. Paintings of different countries reflect different social backgrounds and national styles. According to their subjects, oil paintings can be divided into history paintings, religious paintings, portrait paintings, landscape paintings, still life, genre paintings and so on.

书 法
Chinese Calligraphy

王羲之是举世闻名的中国书法家，《兰亭序》是他的代表作，有"天下第一行书"之称。东晋永和九年（353）三月三日，王羲之与谢安等41人在会稽山下的兰亭宴饮集会。这是一次风雅集会，曲水流觞①、饮酒赋诗，王羲之酒酣之际写下了《兰亭序》。

王羲之的"天下第一行书"——《兰亭序》
Preface of the Orchid Pavilion by Wang Xizhi, renowned as "the best running hand all around the world"

Preface of the Orchid Pavilion is a representative work of Wang Xizhi, a world-famous Chinese calligrapher, and called "the best running hand all around the world". On March 3rd during the ninth year of Emperor Yonghe's reign (353) in the Eastern Jin Dynasty, Wang Xizhi, Xie An and 39 other people held a banquet together at the foot of Kuaiji Mountain. In this tasteful gathering, people sat by the riverside and composed poems while drinking (*qu shui liu shang*① in Chinese) and Wang Xizhi wrote *Preface of the Orchid Pavilion* when he was drinking to his heart's content.

中国书法驰名世界，我们可以从性质、渊源、美学特征、表现手法等方面来欣赏中国书法，它体现了万事万物"对立统一"的基本规律，也反映了人作为万物之灵的精神与气质。

The world-famous Chinese calligraphy can be appreciated from its nature, origin, aesthetic features, and performance characteristics. It reveals the basic law of unity of the opposites in the universe and reflects the spirit and temperament of human beings as the wisest of all creatures.

---

①曲水流觞：大家坐在溪流两旁，在上流放置酒杯，酒杯顺流而下，停在谁的面前，谁就取杯饮酒并作诗。

① *Qu shui liu shang*: sitting by the two sides of river, people put the drinking cup on the upper reach so that the cup flows with the water. The person who is at the place where the cup stops needs to take the cup for drinking and compose a poem.

随着汉字的变化，中国书法也在变化，出现了各种书体，主要有五种：

第一，篆书。一般指小篆，是秦始皇统一文字所用的书体，汉代（前206—公元220）沿用，文字已规范化，偏旁有固定的形式和位置，空虚之处尽量用笔画填满。

第二，隶书。产生于战国（前475—前221），盛行于汉代，打破了篆书曲屈圆转的形体结构，笔画比较平直，魏晋（220—420）以后隶书的正统地位被楷书取代，多用于匾额、碑石。

汉代隶书《乙瑛碑》
Official script in the Han Dynasty—Stele of Yi Ying

第三，楷书。字形方正，是在汉末八分书①的基础上演变而成的新

Along with the changes of Chinese characters, Chinese calligraphy also underwent some changes and different calligraphic styles came into existence. There are five main categories:

First, is the seal script. Generally referring to small seal characters, they were adopted by the First Emperor of the Qin Dynasty with the purpose of standardizing the script. It was still used in the Han Dynasty (206 BC-AD 220) when characters were already standardized. At that time, the Chinese character components had fixed form and place and the blank space was filled with strokes as much as possible.

Second, is the official script. Originating from the Warring States Period (475-221 BC) and prevailing in the Han Dynasty, it is straight in the line strokes, which is different from the curved shape of the seal script. After the Wei and Jin dynasties (220-420) when regular script replaced official script as the legitimate character style, official script was often used in horizontal inscribed boards and steles.

Third, is the regular script. Square in shape, it is a new calligraphic style evolving from *ba fen* style[1] at the end of the Han Dynasty. It prevailed all around the country in the Three Kingdoms (220-280) and underwent new developments in calligraphic style in the Sui and Tang dynasties (581-907). The masterpieces include *Multi-pagoda Stele* by Yan Zhenqing of the Tang Dynasty and *Note of Fushen Temple* by Zhao Mengfu of the Yuan Dynasty. Regular script is still in use today as the standard character writing format.

---

① 八分书：东汉王次仲创造，据说是割程邈隶字的八分取二分，割李斯小篆的二分取八分，故名八分，后演变成为今天的楷书。

[1] *Ba fen* style: created by Wang Cizhong in the Eastern Han Dynasty. It is said that it is called *ba fen* (eighty percent) because it adopts twenty percent of Cheng Miao's official script and eighty percent of Li Si's seal script. Later, it evolved into today's regular script.

书体，三国（220—280）时通行全国，隋唐（581—907）以后在书法风格上有了新的发展，代表作如唐代颜真卿的《多宝塔碑》、元代赵孟頫的《福神观记》等。楷书一直作为正体字沿用至今。

[唐] 颜真卿的《多宝塔碑》拓本
[Tang Dynasty] The rubbing of Multi-pagoda Stele by Yan Zhenqing

第四，草书。特点是笔画相连，书写迅捷，初成于汉代，是为求简便在隶书的基础上产生的。草书笔势流畅、风格潇洒，极具艺术性和美感，代表作如唐代怀素的《自叙帖》、清代邓石如的《五言诗轴》等。

[明] 刘若宰的《草书五言诗扇》
[Ming Dynasty] Fan of a Poem with Five Characters to a Line in Cursive Script by Liu Ruozai

第五，行书。指介于正体字①和

Fourth, is the cursive script. It appears in the Han Dynasty on the basis of seal script for convenience, featuring letters that are joined in a rapid flowing style. Cursive script is extremely artistic and beautiful with its fluent handwriting and natural style. The master works include *Autobiography* by Huai Su in the Tang Dynasty and *Scroll of Poems with Five Characters to a Line* by Deng Shiru in the Qing Dynasty.

Fifth, is the running script. It refers to the flowing calligraphic style between *zhengti* characters[1] and cursive script. It is easy to write and not as difficult to recognize as cursive script. Since the Han Dynasty, running script has undergone some changes in character forms and calligraphic styles with the development of *zhengti* characters. It became the most well-adapted calligraphic style with the widest range of applications as well as the longest duration. Among the works of running script, the most well-known ones are the *Preface of the Orchid Pavilion* by Wang Xizhi in the Jin Dynasty and *Poem Written during the Cold Food Festival in Huangzhou* by Su Shi in the Song Dynasty.

As a form of art, Chinese calligraphy began in

---

①正体字：指在特定时代及范围内使用的符合标准或规范的文字。

① *Zhengti* character: refers to the standardized characters in certain era or particular scope.

草书之间的流畅书体，既便于书写，又不像草书那样难于辨认。从汉代起，行书随着正体字的发展而在体势、笔意上有所变化，成为适应性最强、应用范围最广、延续时间最长的书体，晋代王羲之的《兰亭序》、宋代苏东坡的《黄州寒食诗帖》最为著名。

中国书法作为艺术始于春秋战国，成熟于秦汉，在魏晋南北朝时达到炉火纯青的境界，人们将"汉文、晋字、唐诗、宋词、元曲"相提并论，足见晋字成就之高。书圣王羲之便产生在这个时代，并流传着一个有趣的故事：王羲之注重师法自然，他说鹅是"禽中豪杰，白如雪，洁如玉，一尘不染"，便喜欢观察鹅的动态以揣摩自己的运笔。一天清晨王羲

the Spring and Autumn Period and the Warring States Period, and matured in the Qin and Han dynasties and reached high perfection in the Wei, Jin, Northern and Southern dynasties. The great achievement of calligraphy in the Jin Dynasty is obvious because articles of the Han Dynasty, calligraphy of the Jin Dynasty, poetry of the Tang Dynasty, *ci* of the Song Dynasty and *qu* of the Yuan Dynasty are always mentioned in the same breath. Wang Xizhi, known as "the saint of calligraphy", lived in this age. An interesting story goes like this: Wang Xizhi stressed getting inspiration from nature and said that goose "is the hero of poultry because it is spotless, as white as snow and as clean as jade". Therefore, he loved to observe the movements of goose to think about how to wield his writing brush. One morning when Wang enjoyed the landscape scenery on boat top, he was unconsciously absorbed in

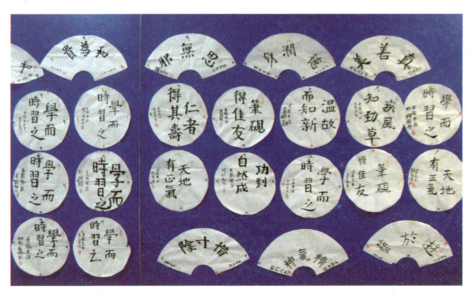

北京语言大学汉语学院留学生书法习作
Exercises in calligraphy by foreign students from College of Chinese Studies in Beijing Language and Culture University

之乘船观赏山水，不觉对岸边一群白鹅看得出神，便想买回去，鹅的主人是一位道士，他说："倘若大人想要，就请给我写一部道家养生修炼的《黄庭经》吧！"王羲之求鹅心切，便应允了，用他的书法换了白鹅。

时至今日，中国人依然热爱着书法，使用着书法。古老的书法不仅魅力不减，而且吸引着许许多多的外国人，无论是中国汉语国际教育的课堂，还是海外孔子学院的文化活动，都离不开书法的展示、讲解与练习，现在书法已成为中外文化交流的一种重要媒介。

watching the white geese on the opposite bank and wanted to buy these geese. The owner of the geese was a Taoist priest who said that "if you want to get the geese, please write for me *The Yellow Court Classic* as for Taoists to keep in good health!" Wang Xizhi was so desperate to get the geese that he agreed and exchanged his calligraphy for the white geese.

Even to this day, Chinese people still love and use calligraphy. The old calligraphy does not lose its charm but attracts many foreigners. Calligraphy display, explanation and practice are seen both in international education courses of Chinese characters and in cultural events in Confucius Institutes overseas. Nowadays calligraphy has become an important medium of cultural communication between China and other countries.

三言两语 A FEW REMARKS

学习书法不是功利的事情，不是可有可无的事情，而是中国人起码的义务。拿好毛笔，练好中国汉字，才是一个中国人最根本的文化风度、文化脸面。没有了这条，就谈不上国家的文化安全。把书法当作艺术来欣赏就是小看了它。书法不是艺术选修课，而应该跟幼儿教育、认字同步进行。

[中国] 孙晓云，女，书法家

对于我来说，书法有点儿难，因为我的母语是阿拉伯语，完全不一样。中国书法具有悠久的历史，据我所知，书法是来源于自然与生活的，我觉得特别有意思。但是书法很难，需要很努力地练习才能学好，不过会越学越有兴趣。

[苏丹] 哈默图，男，大学生

Learning calligraphy is not utilitarian or dispensable but a fundamental duty for Chinese people. Taking the writing brush and practicing calligraphy is a basic cultural manner and a way of getting self-respect for Chinese. Without this, national cultural security is out of the question. Treating calligraphy as an art for admiration belittles it. Calligraphy should be learned at the same time as preschool education and basic reading education instead of being listed as an elective art course.

[China] Sun Xiaoyun, female, calligrapher

Calligraphy is a bit difficult for me because my native language of Arabic is completely different. According to my knowledge, calligraphy has a long history and comes from nature and life, which is quite interesting for me. However, calligraphy is so difficult that one needs to make great efforts in practice. But one will be more interested in it through the process of learning it.

[Sudan] Hammerton, male, university student

空海铜像　*The bronze statue of Kukai*

中国书法伴随汉字和汉文化传入日本，在日本被消化、吸收与再创造，日本佛教高僧空海作出了重要贡献。空海公元804年（中国的唐朝时期）来到中国学习密宗，806年回国创立真言宗。他既是汉字书法的积极传播者，又另辟蹊径，大胆采用汉字草书作平假名，将书法诸要素有机地统一在一起。1975年，日本奈良市将空海所书《伊吕波歌》原拓赠送给北京故宫博物院，它是中日书法艺术交流的历史见证。

Chinese calligraphy was introduced into Japan together with Chinese characters and culture. The Japanese Buddhist monk Kukai made a great contribution to the digestion, absorption and recreation of Chinese calligraphy in Japan. Kukai visited China in 804 (during the Tang Dynasty in China) to learn Tantra and established Shingon Esoteric sect of Buddhism back in Japan in 806. He not only actively spread Chinese calligraphy but also found a new path that he boldly used Chinese cursive script in hiragana writing and organically unified various elements in calligraphy. In 1975, the Nara City in Japan sent the original rubbing of Kukai's *Iroha Song* to the Palace Museum in Beijing as testimony of the history of Sino-Japanese calligraphy communication.

印 章
Chinese Seal

印 章

2010年6月26日，在台湾宇珍国际艺术有限公司举办的拍卖会上，清"乾隆青玉螭龙玉玺"以新台币4.8250亿元（约1500万美元）成交，拍出了天价。乾隆皇帝非常喜爱印章，一生刻制的宝玺达一千八百余方，多半以玉制作，此次拍卖的"青玉螭龙玉玺"印面是正方形，以汉文篆书刻着"乾隆御览之宝"六个大字，螭龙钮中的螭龙神态威猛。

和阗青玉制成的"乾隆青玉螭龙玉玺"
The Greenish Jade Dragon Seal from the Qianlong Period was made with greenish jade from Khotan.

In the audition held by Taiwan Yu Jen International Art and Antique Co., Ltd. on June 26th in 2010, the *Greenish Jade Dragon Seal* in Qianlong Period of the Qing Dynasty was bid in with a sky-high price—NTD 482.5 million (about USD 15 million). Emperor Qianlong loved seals so much that he had over 1,800 seals carved in his lifetime and most of them were made with jade. The bottom of the *Greenish Jade Dragon Seal* is square with "乾隆御览之宝" (treasure enjoyed by Emperor Qianlong) in the official script of the Han Dynasty carved on it. The dragon on the upper part of the seal is quite strong and formidable.

印章是印于文件、书画上表示签署或鉴定的文具，制作材质主要有金属、木头、石头（包括玉石）等。

中国最古老的雕刻文字有商朝的甲骨文、周朝的钟鼎文、秦朝的刻石等。古代镌刻文字的钟鼎和碑碣等

The seal is a tool to be stamped on documents, paintings or calligraphy showing signing or authentication. It is mainly made of metal, wood, stone (including jade), etc.

The oldest inscribed characters in China include oracle bone inscriptions from the Shang Dynasty, inscriptions on ancient bronze

通称为"金石"，印章即包括在"金石"里。中国印章至迟出现于周朝，开始时只是作为商业上交流货物的凭证。秦始皇统一中国后，印章的范围扩大为证明当权者权益的法物，后来也成为皇帝与贵族闲暇时的玩物，至清朝发展到极致，今天则是人们用来修身养性的物件。

[清] 乾隆年间的"内府图书"象牙印章
[Qing Dynasty] The ivory seal "内府图书" (the book belonging to the imperial storehouse) carved on it from Qianlong Period

　　印章种类繁多，基本上可分为官印和私印两类。官印即官方使用的印章，历代官印各有规定，不仅名称不同，形状、大小、印文、纽式也有差异。私印是对官印以外印章的统称，体制复杂，可以从字面意义、制作方法、治印材料、构成形式上分成各种类别。

objects in the Zhou Dynasty, and stone inscriptions from the Qin Dynasty. The ancient bronze objects and stone tablets used for character inscription are collectively known as *jinshi* and the seal is a kind of *jinshi*. Chinese seals appeared no later than the Zhou Dynasty and served as evidence of business trade in goods. After the First Emperor of the Qin Dynasty unified China, seals were more widely applied and became the legitimate object to prove the authority's rights. Later, they were also used as the plaything of emperors and aristocrats in their leisure time. They reached their full development in the Qing Dynasty and become the objects for people's self-cultivation today.

Among the great variety of seals, official seals and private seals are the basic two kinds. Official seals, used by officials, have different standards in different dynasties and differ from each other in names, shapes, sizes, words at the bottom of them and sculpted decorations on the upper part of them. Seals except for official ones are jointly called private seals. They have a complex system and can be

形形色色的印章　*Various seals*

中国历代文学家与书画家都对印章情有独钟，许多印人也擅长诗书画，他们常常取用一些典故成语、诗词佳句或者俚俗语言作为闲章内容，往往能出奇制胜，饶有情趣和意味。当我们鉴赏到这类语句时，也会觉得分外地有滋有味、兴趣盎然。

自明清以来，印章作为书画的重要组成部分，已成为定式。一个全面的画家，应该有书画的理论，通晓书法、画法、篆刻，而且具有娴熟的技法。一些著名的书画家即是这样，如赵孟頫、齐白石等。他们不仅精书画，而且自己也会治印，由此他们制作的印章更能与自己的绘画作品相配

赵孟頫《红衣罗汉》（辽宁省博物馆藏）
Arhat in Red Dress by Zhao Mengfu (reserved in Liaoning Provincial Museum)

合，达到更完美的和谐、统一。

divided into various groups based on their literal meanings, manufacturing methods, production materials, and constructing components.

Litterateurs and artists in all periods of Chinese history show special preference for seals. Quite many seal makers are also good at calligraphy and painting and often use literary quotations, idioms, excellent poems, slangs and folk adages as the contents of unofficial personal seals. Thus, they achieve success in this unique way and create much fun and significance at the same time. While appreciating these kinds of words and sentences, we Chinese also feel that they are immensely interesting.

Since the Ming and Qing dynasties, seals have become a fixed and important part of paintings and calligraphy. A well-rounded painter should master not only the theories and techniques of painting, calligraphy and seal cutting, but also consummate skills. Some famous painters and calligraphers are proficient in calligraphy and painting and capable of making seals such as Zhao Mengfu and Qi Baishi. Their seals and paintings match well with each other and realize harmony, unity and perfection.

三言两语 A FEW REMARKS

印章在古代就是一种信用器物，是一个人品行和德操的证明。印章石经过篆刻家和雕刻家的雕刻之后，就由一颗石头变成了一件具有文化意义的艺术品。章文是印章的灵魂，是印章的价值体现。例如，"穆如清风"四个字就是指和美的事物如清风一样滋养万物，教育人们要守住清廉，培养个人的高尚德行。

[中国] 孙启勤，男，印章收藏家

我来中国留学是因为我对在中国餐馆看到的汉字非常好奇，我的母语是拼音文字，可汉字不知道是怎么念出来的，更像一幅画，我想知道汉字的秘密，就来到了中国。到了中国以后我对印章特别感兴趣，我觉得它像书法一样是纯粹的汉字的艺术，而且是一种可以随时带在身上的艺术品。

[安提瓜和巴布达] 巴布朗，男，大学生

In ancient China, the seal was a symbol of credit that proved one's behavior and character. The seal made of stone was transformed into a work of art with cultural significance after being engraved by seal cutting experts and sculptors. As the soul of the seal, the words on it reveal the seal's value. For instance, "穆如清风" means that harmonious and beautiful things nourish everything like the cool breeze, teaching people to keep integrity while also training individuals' lofty character.

[China] Sun Qiqin, male, seal collector

I came to study in China because I was curious about the Chinese characters that I saw in Chinese restaurants. My native language has an alphabetic system of writing and I had no idea about how Chinese characters were read because they were quite similar to pictures. I wanted to explore the secrets of Chinese characters and therefore came to China. After arriving in China, I developed great interest in seals which, in my opinion, is a pure art form of Chinese characters like calligraphy as well as a work of art that you can carry with you.

[Antigua and Barbuda] Barbrown, male, university student

小链接 ADDITIONAL INFORMATION

欧洲的纹章
Coat of arms in Europe

纹章（Coat of Arms）指一种按照特定规则构成的标志，是专属于某个个人、家族或团体的识别物。欧洲中古时代就有自己的纹章体系，当时也称盾章，主要是为了识别因披挂盔甲而无法辨认真实面目的骑士。有一段时间纹章成为贵族的专利，从13世纪起，无论是贵族还是平民，只要遵守相关规则，都可以拥有和使用纹章，至今它仍然可以作为识别个人、机构、企业等的世袭或继承性标记。

The coat of arms, which refers to the sign formed according to certain rules, is a symbol which belongs exclusively to certain individuals, families or groups. During the middle ages, Europe already had its own system for a coat of arms (also known as coat armory at that time) whose main purpose was to recognize the knights who cannot be identified when they wear armor. There was a period of time when the coat of arms was monopolized by aristocrats. Since the 13th century, both aristocrats and ordinary people could possess and use the coat of arms as long as they abided by the rules. At present, the coat of arms is still employed as a hereditary or inherited symbol to recognize individuals, institutions and enterprises.

Living in China

生活在中国

胡同与四合院
Hutong and Siheyuan

什刹海，田琨摄
Shicha Lake, photographed by Tian Kun

北京城里有一片难得的水域，叫"什刹海"，由西海、后海、前海等水面组成，是元大都水系的一部分。什刹海周围分布着许多胡同和四合院，有庙宇、王府、民居等等，是北京重要的历史文化保护街区。

Shicha Lake, comprising Xihai (West Lake), Houhai (Rear Lake) and Qianhai (Front Lake), is a precious water area in Beijing City, as well as part of the water system of the capital city of the Yuan Dynasty. Surrounding the Shicha Lake are many *hutong*s (allies) and *siheyuan*s (Chinese quadrangles) including temples, princes' dwellings and civil residences, which altogether form an important block for the preservation of history and culture.

"胡同"这个词元代就有了，后来成为"小巷"的代名词。胡同的产生与发展和元大都的规划设计有着密切的关系。在北京，自元代保留至今的一条胡同是南锣鼓巷，这是一条南北走向的古老街巷，北接鼓楼东大街，南至地安门东大街，东西两侧各有八条古老的胡同，形成极有北京历史文化特色的胡同与四合院民居群。

四合院是中国最典型的民居建筑，是由四面房屋围合起来的一种内院式住宅。四合院的大门是等级和地

The word *hutong* has existed since the Yuan Dynasty and later became a synonym for *xiaoxiang* (small alley). The emergence and

南锣鼓巷，田琨摄
The South Luogu Lane, photographed by Tian Kun

四合院的大门，田琨摄
Gate of a siheyuan, photographed by Tian Kun

位的象征，往往有着华丽的装饰。门墩是支撑四合院大门的石头，又叫"抱鼓石"，上面常雕刻着狮子等吉祥图案。门簪是装在大门上方的木质构件，一般有两个或四个，门簪上常有"吉祥如意"、"福禄寿喜"等汉字，也有蝙蝠、仙鹤等动物图案，以表达四合院主人对生活的美好愿望。

700多年来，数以千计的胡同与不同形态的四合院为古老的北京留下许多故事，而胡同里渐去渐远的叫卖声也成为老北京人心中永远的回忆。2002年，北京市公布了25片历史文化保护区，使北京城区部分胡同和四合院得到较为完整的保存。除什刹海地区和南锣鼓巷外，还有西四北头条

development of the *hutong* was closely related to the city design of the capital of Yuan Dynasty. Built in the Yuan Dynasty, the *hutong* South Luogu Lane in Beijing is still well-preserved to present day. Being oriented to south and north, the ancient alley joins Gulou East Street in the north and extends to Di'anmen East Street in the south; it is respectively flanked by eight ancient *hutong*s on the east and south sides, forming a residence complex of *hutong*s and *siheyuan*s which embodies the rich historical and cultural characteristics of Beijing.

Siheyuan, the most typical residence in China, is a kind of courtyard residence surrounded by houses along the four sides. Bearing ornate decorations in most cases, the gate of a *siheyuan* symbolizes social rank and status. The stone pillars supporting the gate of a *siheyuan* are often referred to as "drum-shaped supporting stones", and are usually carved with auspicious patterns like lions. Gate cylinders are wooden components fixed above the door; and generally there are two or four of them. Chinese characters such as "吉祥如意" (auspicious and lucky) and "福禄寿喜" (good fortune, wealth, longevity, happiness), etc. are often engraved on the gate cylinders; there are also designs of animals like bats and cranes on the cylinders to show the courtyard owner's good wishes towards life.

For over 700 years, thousands of *hutong*s and *siheyuan*s with various layouts have left behind endless stories of the ancient Beijing City; peddlers' voices gradually fading away in *hutong*s has become an eternal memory in the

至八条、东四三条至八条等。20世纪
90年代以来，也有一部分曾经是"大
杂院"的四合院经过更新改造之后成
为新式四合院民居，如南锣鼓巷东边
菊儿胡同里的四合院。

北京的胡同，田琨摄
Hutong in Beijing, photographed by Tian Kun

　　如果你想了解北京的历史，体
验北京传统文化与现代生活的融合，
就去寻访已为数不多的胡同和四合院
吧。行走在幽深的胡同中，你会不知
不觉地忘却现代都市的喧嚣与浮躁，
重拾往昔的宁静与安详。

minds of the natives of old Beijing. In 2002, Beijing City published a list containing 25 historical and cultural protection zones, which guaranteed the fairly complete preservation of some *hutong*s and *siheyuan*s in the city area of Beijing. These include Shicha Lake area, South Luogu Lane, the 1st to the 8th alleys of Xisi North, and the 3rd to the 8th alleys of Dongsi. Starting from the 1990s, some compounds formerly occupied by many households went through a series of renovation and reconstruction, forming a new kind of *siheyuan*s, for example, the ones located in the Ju'er Hutong east of South Luogu Lane.

　If you want to learn the history of Beijing and experience its combination of traditional culture and modern life, just go and explore those few remaining *hutong*s and *siheyuan*s. Walking along the endless and quiet *hutong*s, you will unconsciously forget the hustle and bustle of the modern metropolis and regain long lost serenity and tranquility.

我是城市规划专业的学生，我觉得胡同与四合院所特有的文化价值，在于它是北京历史名城延续数百年的传统文化的载体，应该有重点地保留一些相对完整的四合院，它是历史的活化石。

[中国] 武筝，男，大学生

我从小在老北京的四合院中长大，四合院很敞亮，不但环境优雅安逸，而且住户往往是小康之家，生活比较祥和安定，有点儿文化情趣。上初中时我家和老邻居都陆续迁进了楼房。爱花的不能多养了，爱鱼的只好把大鱼缸换成小鱼罐，而在自家院子里享受轻风拂过绿荫的感觉再也找不到了。现在老邻居们偶尔碰到一起，还会陶醉地回忆起住在四合院的时光。

[中国] 许卫民，男，工人

住在四合院，给我的感觉是精致、文雅，这种感受很深刻，特别是在晚上。四合院的晚上最有意思，比白天还有意思，特别静。在这种安静里，你会比较放松；在放松的状态里，你可以把问题想得比较清楚。我经常晚上不睡觉，写东西。

[美国] 龙志安，男，律师

I'm a student majoring in city planning. In my opinion, the unique cultural value of *hutong*s and *siheyuan*s lies in the fact that they are the carriers of traditional culture extending for hundreds of years in historically honored Beijing. We should give priority to the preservation of some relatively complete *siheyuan*s, because they are the living fossils of our history.

[China] Wu Zheng, male, university student

I grow up in the *siheyuan*s of old Beijing. They are spacious, well-lit and possess an elegant and comfortable environment. What's more, its residents are often fairly well-off households living a happy and peaceful life, which adds to a taste of culture. My family and old neighbors gradually moved to apartments when I entered junior high school. Since then, I could no longer raise as many favorite flowers as I wished; I had to replace my big fishbowl with a smaller one; what's more, I could no longer feel the gentle breeze blowing across the tree shade. Even up to now, when old neighbors occasionally run across each other, they still indulge themselves in the nostalgia of old times when everybody lived together in the *siheyuan*s.

[China] Xu Weimin, male, worker

Living in a *siheyuan*, I experience a strong feeling of delicacy and grace, especially at nights. The nights in a *siheyuan* are the most fascinating, much more superb than during the day, for they are extremely quiet. Under such tranquility, you will reach a high degree of relaxation which helps you to think over problems very clearly. I often stay up at night to write about something.

[United States] Long Zhian, male, lawyer

"三坊一照壁"是白族民居的主要形式。"三坊"指由一面正房和两面厢房组成的三面房屋，一般是三间两层。照壁指正房对面的影壁，三面房屋与一面照壁构成一个封闭式院落。门楼和照壁是白族民居中最富有民族特色的部分，多以青石或大理石为材料，门

白族民居
Bai people's residence

楼中间镶嵌大理石浮雕，上面飞檐斗拱，造型优美典雅。门楼与照壁的装饰多采用木雕、砖雕、泥塑、彩绘、石刻、大理石拼镶等手法，工艺精湛，手法细腻，充分体现了白族人民的审美传统和聪明才智。

The residence of Bai people are typically characterized by "three *fang*s and one *zhaobi*". "Three *fang*s" refer to the three-sided, usually two-story high compound consisting of a main house and two side houses. *Zhaobi* is a screen wall facing the main house, which combines with the houses on three sides to form an enclosure for the courtyard. Built mainly with bluestones and marbles, the gateway arch and the screen wall embody the richest ethnic feature of the Bai people's dwellings. Marble sculptures in relief are embedded in the middle of the gateway arch. Over the arch, the upturned eaves display a graceful appearance. Decorative methods such as woodcarving, brick cutting, clay sculpting, color painting, stone engraving and marble inlay, etc. are applied to the gateway arch and screen wall. They require exquisite craftsmanship and delicate skills, which substantially reflect the Bai people's aesthetic tradition and intelligence.

玩 偶
Dolls

图片中胖墩墩的娃娃是中国有名的泥玩偶，产于江苏惠山，被称为"大阿福"。它的样子十分喜庆、可爱，常常怀抱狮子、麒麟或鲤鱼，在民间是迎福纳祥、辟邪祛灾的吉祥物。

Made in Huishan, Jiangsu Province, the two chubby children in the picture are famous clay dolls in China; and they are called Da Ah Fu. The jubilant and cute doll, often carrying a lion or a Chinese unicorn or a carp in its bosom, is regarded as a mascot welcoming happiness and warding off misfortunes.

大阿福
Da Ah Fu

玩偶是中国民间艺术的一个重要门类，一般用泥土、陶瓷、绒布等材料制成。它们既是孩子们手中的玩具，也是中国人家居辟邪的物品，其名称和样式因民族、地域等差异而不同，以北京为例，就有兔儿爷、毛猴、鬃人等等。

在中国民间神话传说中有一位月亮女神，名叫"嫦娥"，住在月宫里，陪伴她的是一只会捣药的玉兔。过去，玉兔是中秋节时人们供奉和祭拜的对象，老北京人尊称它为"兔儿

Dolls form an important branch of Chinese folk art; which are usually made of materials such as clay, pottery, flannelette and so on. They are not only toys for children, but also objects used to avoid evil spirits. The names and shapes of dolls vary according to specific ethnic and regional differences. Take dolls in Beijing for example, there are the master hare doll, the hairy monkey doll and the *zongren* doll (a human doll with pig's bristles stuck to its base).

According to Chinese folk mythology, Chang'e, goddess of the moon resides in the moon palace. She was accompanied by a jade hare who is able to pound medicine. In the

爷"。"爷"，是封建时代人们对地位高贵者的尊称，后来引申为对神的尊称。老北京的兔儿爷是用泥塑成的，身穿战袍，头戴帽盔，骑在老虎身上，威风凛凛，是老北京中秋节的代表形象。

兔儿爷
Master hare doll

在北京还有一种绝妙的传统民间工艺品，叫"毛猴"。制作毛猴的材料主要来自大自然中的植物和动物，它们同时也是两种中药材，一种叫"辛夷"，即玉兰花的花骨朵，用来做毛猴的身体；另一种叫"蝉蜕"，即知了的壳，用来做毛猴的头和四肢。毛猴作品反映了北京的民俗传统与社会生活，也体现了北京人的智慧和生活情趣。

past, people enshrined and worshipped the jade hare during the Mid-autumn Festival, and people in old Beijing honored it as "兔儿爷" (master hare). "爷" (master) was a respectful form of address for people with high status, and was later extended as an honorable title for gods. Molded from clay, the master hare is a representative figure during the Mid-autumn Festival in old Beijing; it is dressed in a war robe and wearing a helmet; the hare rides on a tiger and appears immensely majestic.

There is another kind of extraordinary traditional folk handicraft in Beijing—the hairy monkey doll. The materials employed in the making of hairy monkey dolls are gathered from natural plants and animals. These materials are also two kinds of traditional Chinese medicines, one is called *xinyi*, flower buds of magnolia which are used to make the body of a monkey; the other is called *chantui*, namely the slough of cicada which is employed to make the monkey's head and limbs. The hairy monkey dolls not only reflect the tradition of folk customs and social life in Beijing, but also display Beijingers' wisdom and taste for life.

There once existed a kind of doll named *zongren* in Beijing. Emerging in the last years of the Qing Dynasty,

毛猴作品"下棋"
Handicraft of hairy monkey dolls, Playing Chinese Chess

过去北京还有一种被称为"鬃人"的玩偶，创始于清朝末年，是受皮影和京剧的影响而产生的，曾经盛极一时。鬃人用泥、纸布和绸绢做成，在底座上粘有一圈猪鬃。把鬃人放在铜盘上，不断敲打铜盘，由于受到震动，鬃人会凭借鬃毛的弹性在铜盘上来回转动，好像在舞台上表演，所以又被称为"盘中戏"。1915年，由著名民间艺人王春佩、王汉卿父子制作的鬃人曾获巴拿马万国博览会银质奖章。

北京以外，中国各地都有很多用布做成的动物玩偶，布老虎是其中的代表。布老虎来源于中国民间对虎的崇拜。老虎是一种威猛的动物，在狮子传入中国以前一直被人们认为是百兽之王。中国民间有给小孩子戴虎头帽、穿虎头鞋的习俗，认为可以保佑孩子健康平安。在汉语中，人们常用"虎头虎脑"

the doll was influenced by shadow play and Beijing opera, and had prevailed for some time. *Zongren* dolls are made of clay, paper cloth and silk with a circle of pig bristles stuck to their base. Placing the *zongren* dolls on the bronze plate, people would strike the plate without stopping; under the vibration caused by the strike, the dolls would revolve to and fro on the plate as a result of the elasticity of bristles, looking as if performing on the stage. Thus the performance is also called a "play on the plate". *Zongren* dolls made by the folk artists Wang Chunpei and his son Wang Hanqing won the silver medal during the 1915 Panama Pacific International Exposition.

Outside Beijing, there are also many animal dolls made of cloth in every part of China, among them the cloth tiger is the representative one. The cloth tiger emerged as a result of Chinese folk worship of tigers. As a kind of ferocious animal, the tiger is deemed as the king of all animals before the lion was introduced into China. According to Chinese folk custom, people would dress children in hats and shoes decorated with cloth tiger heads, thinking that they are able to bless children with health. In the Chinese language, a robust child is often described with the idiom "虎头虎脑" (literally, tiger head and tiger mind), and a vigorous young person with "生龙活虎" (literally a lively dragon and an active tiger). Chinese folks believe that tigers have the capability of guarding the house,

布老虎
Cloth tigers

形容小孩子身体长得结实强壮，或用"生龙活虎"形容年轻人富有朝气。中国百姓认为老虎还有看家护财、镇宅辟邪的作用。布老虎一般由妇女手工缝制，颜色形态丰富多样，充分反映了制作者的聪明才智与审美观念，因而深受人们喜爱。

protecting the wealth, stabilizing the family and warding off misfortunes. Cloth tigers are usually sewn by craftswomen. Made in a wide variety of colors and shapes, tiger cloth reflects the wisdom and aesthetic taste of craftsmen, and thus is greatly adored by people.

三言两语 A FEW REMARKS

我给我女儿买过好多玩偶，大部分是漂亮的娃娃。现在的孩子都是独生子女，有的时候没有可以一起玩耍的伙伴就和她的娃娃一起玩儿。我女儿经常给她的娃娃梳头发、做衣服，我觉得这样也能培养她的爱心和动手能力。

[中国] 郑玉婷，女，记者

I've bought many dolls for my daughter, and most of them are beautiful children's dolls. Now, every child is the only kid in his/her family, and my daughter plays with her dolls when she cannot find playmates. My daughter often combs hairs and makes clothes for her dolls, which I believe is a way of developing her sense of care and hand skills.

[China] Zheng Yuting, female, journalist

玩偶做到价值1000元以上，就是一件上好的工艺品了。相比小孩子玩的普通玩偶，进口高端玩偶胜在"高保真"。除了关节精致到连手指头都可以动以外，这些玩偶穿的皮衣、皮鞋也都是真皮制作的。当一双鞋子被要求缩小到半个小指头大时，这些皮鞋上的鞋带也不是画上去的，而是人工一针一线穿上去的，太精致了。

[中国] 徐欣，男，玩偶店老板

Once a doll reaches a value of more than 1,000 RMB, it can be regarded as a superior handicraft. Compared with ordinary dolls for children, imported dolls are outstanding in terms of their "high fidelity". Their joints are so delicate that even the fingers can move, and the leather clothes and shoes are genuine ones. When a pair of shoes is minified to the size of a half finger, the laces are still sewn using needles and threads instead of drawings. This appears so exquisite.

[China] Xu Xin, male, owner of a dolls shop

我喜欢做手工，用棉布、木头、泥土、稻草等做材料，可以制作出许多漂亮、可爱的人物和动物。我认为这些玩偶是有灵性的，所以我给我制作的每一个玩偶都起了名字，让他们成为一个大家族，而我就是族长。当送给亲戚、朋友"领养"时，我还真有点儿舍不得呢。

[荷兰] 安妮，女，家庭主妇

I love handicrafts because I can make lots of beautiful, cute figures and animals with materials such as cotton cloth, wood, clay and straw. In my opinion, these dolls are endowed with life, so I named every doll I made and regard them as part of a big family in which I am the clan head. When I send them as presents to my relatives and friends for "adoption", I'm really loath to part with them.

[Netherlands] Annie, female, housewife

小链接 ADDITIONAL INFORMATION

　　偶人节又称"女儿节"，是日本的传统节日，在历史上曾受到中国古代上巳节风俗的影响，源于古时人们在水边驱除污秽厄运、祈求健康平安的活动。早在平安时代（794—1192），日本贵族女性中即流行赏玩偶人的习俗，人们相信把偶人和供物放在水中任其漂流，可以把疾病和灾难带走。后来偶人的制作越来越精致，种类也越来越多。江户时代（1603—1867），每年3月3日被正式定为"偶人节"。节日期间精致的木偶娃娃被人们摆在家中观赏，节日过后又精心地收藏起来。后来，"偶人节"演变为一种祈盼女孩子健康、幸福的节日。

日本的偶人，刘谦功摄
Japanese dolls, photographed by Liu Qiangong

Hinamatsuri (Dolls' Day), also known as Girls' Day is a traditional Japanese festival which was once influenced by the ancient Chinese Shangsi Festival when people gathered together near the waterside to wash away dirtiness and misfortunes and pray for health and safety. As early as the Heian period (794-1192), the custom of appreciating the dolls became popular among Japanese noblewomen. People believed that by setting dolls and offerings afloat on the water and letting them drift, they would take illness and disasters away. As time went on, the dolls were more and more exquisitely made with ever-growing varieties. In the Edo period (1603-1867), March 3rd was officially designated as the Dolls' Day. During the festival, delicate dolls are arranged in houses for people's admiration and will be carefully kept when the festival is over. Later, the Dolls' Day has evolved into a festival of praying for girls' health and happiness.

筷 子
Chopsticks

筷子又称"箸"，是中餐必备的餐具。在汉语中，有不少谚语是用筷子作比喻的，如"一根筷子容易折，一把筷子硬如铁"；"单筷难夹菜，独翅难飞天"。这些谚语都强调了集体的力量，反映了中国的文化特色与民族精神。

龙凤筷子
Chopsticks with patterns of dragon and phoenix

Also known as "箸", chopsticks are essential eating utensils in Chinese meals. In the Chinese language, there are many proverbs using analogies related to chopsticks, such as "one chopstick is easy to be broken, while a bunch of chopsticks are as hard as iron" and "it's difficult to pick up food with a chopstick just as it's hard to soar into the sky with only one wing." All these proverbs emphasize collective power and reflect the characteristics of Chinese culture and national spirit.

在中国，筷子的制作有着非常悠久的历史，其产生来源于以农耕文化为主的生产生活方式。制作筷子的原料南北不同，南方筷子多取材于竹，北方筷子多取材于木。从"筷"字的汉字结构来看，早期的筷子应该是以竹子为主的，因而"筷"和"箸"这两个字都有竹字头。

筷子的优点很多，首先是灵活方便，适于家人围坐在一起的传统饮食方式。其次是可以增强手臂、手指和大脑的灵活性。握筷的方法

China's chopstick-making has enjoyed a long historical standing. The emergence of chopsticks is related to Chinese people's production methods and lifestyle centering on land cultivation. Materials used to make chopsticks vary from south to north: chopsticks in southern China are mostly made from bamboo while those in northern China are usually made from wood. Examining from the construction of the Chinese character "筷"(chopsticks), it is highly probable that early chopsticks were mainly made of bamboo, for the two characters "筷" and "箸" invariably contain the radical "竹" (meaning bamboo).

与使用毛笔一样很有讲究。一般是将筷子尖对齐，用拇指、食指、中指和无名指四根手指轻轻握住筷子，中指放在两根筷子中间，用无名指和虎口稳住里面的一根筷子，再用拇指、食指和中指操纵外面的

握筷子的方法
The proper way of holding chopsticks

另一根筷子。

与西餐的刀叉不同，中餐使用的筷子一定是成双成对的。中国人喜欢双数，而筷子有"好事成双"的寓意。同时"筷子"与"快子"谐音，人们喜欢把筷子送给新婚夫妇，祝愿他们"早生贵子"。

制作筷子的材料十分广泛，传统材质有竹、木、金、银、石、兽骨、象牙等，其中竹木筷子是最普通的一种，此外也有陶瓷筷子和不锈钢筷子等。在现代中国人的生活中，筷子除了被用作餐具和礼品外，也被人们当作艺术品来收藏。在北京有一些传统商业街——如前

Chopsticks come with many advantages. First they are flexible and convenient, and suitable for the traditional way of eating where the whole family sits together around a table. Second, using chopsticks can enhance the flexibility of the arms, fingers and the acuteness of the brain. The method of holding chopsticks is as subtle as holding a brush. Usually, we should first of all adjust the two pointed tips of a pair of chopsticks until they are even with each other; secondly, hold the chopsticks gently using the thumb, index finger, middle finger and ring finger, with the middle finger positioned between the two chopsticks; then maintain the lower chopstick with the ring finger and the part of the hand between the thumb and the index finger, and then employ the thumb, index finger and middle finger to manipulate the higher chopstick.

Different from knives and forks used in western meals, chopsticks used in Chinese meals invariably form pairs. Chinese people love even numbers and chopsticks carry a connotation of "good things in pairs". In the meantime, because "筷子"(chopsticks) is homophonous to "快子" (having babies soon), people like to send chopsticks as presents to newly married couples, wishing them to give birth to precious children as soon as possible.

Chopsticks are made from a wide variety of materials. Traditional materials include bamboo, wood, gold, silver, stone, animal bone and ivory. Bamboo and wooden chopsticks are the most commonly observed ones, besides there are also porcelain and stainless steel chopsticks. In modern Chinese people's life, chopsticks,

礼品筷子
Gift chopsticks

门大栅栏，那里有专门的筷子商店，里面有各式各样的筷子供人们选择。

在亚洲，日本和韩国同属于汉字文化圈，餐桌上也都使用筷子，但日本和韩国的筷子与中国的筷子有明显区别。从形状上来看，中国的筷子一般是上粗下细，上方下圆。日本的筷子比中国的筷子细，以便于夹取米饭和海味；韩国的筷子多用金属制成，以方便食用烧烤类食物。

中国人的餐桌，刘谦功摄
Chinese dining-table, photographed by Liu Qiangong

apart from being used as eating utensils, are also collected as works of art by the public. On some of the traditional commercial avenues in Beijing, for example Dazhalan (colloquially Dashilar) in Qianmen Street, there are shops selling all kinds of chopsticks exclusively.

Japan and Korea in Asia both belong to the Chinese character cultural sphere thus chopsticks are also found on their dining tables. However there are apparent differences among Japanese, Korean and Chinese chopsticks. In terms of the shape, Chinese chopsticks are usually thick and square at the upper ends while thin and round at the tips. Japanese chopsticks are made thinner than Chinese ones to facilitate the picking of rice and seafood. The majority of Korean chopsticks are made from metal, making them more effective for eating during barbecues.

On Chinese dining tables, there are several commonly observed rules of etiquette. For example, the guests should not take up their chopsticks to pick up food until invited by the hosts; in addition, one should not hesitate

在中式宴席上，使用筷子有一些需要共同遵守的礼仪，比如客人不能先动筷子，应该等主人发出邀请之后再夹菜；又如不要在餐桌上举着筷子犹豫不定，不知道选择哪一种菜；再如不能在菜盘中翻来捡去，专挑自己喜欢吃的菜等。入乡随俗，在中国吃饭，最好能遵守中国人吃饭的规矩。

over which dishes to take while holding one's chopsticks above the table; moreover, one should not dig or search through the dishes for one's favorite food. As the saying goes "when in Rome, do as the Romans do", it is always desirable to observe Chinese people's eating etiquette when having meals in China.

三言两语 A FEW REMARKS

关于筷子，我听到过这样一个传说，现在讲给你们听。相传大禹在治理洪水时三过家门而不入，都在野外进餐，有时时间紧迫，刚烧开锅就得吃，吃完好赶路。但汤水太烫无法下手，就折两根树枝夹着吃，这就是筷子的雏形。不管这个传说是真是假，因熟食烫手而使用筷子绝对是有说服力的。

[中国] 方圆，女，教师

I'd like to tell you a story about chopsticks I once heard. According to the ancient story, when Yu the Great was undertaking the water-control project, he didn't enter his home while passing it for three times and had his meals in the wild. Because time was lacking, he had to start eating as soon as the food was cooked and then proceeded with his journey. As the soup was too hot for the hands to pick up food, Yu the Great snapped two twigs from the tree and employed them to take food. These were the early forms of chopsticks. Whether the legend is true or not, it is absolutely persuasive to say that people used chopsticks to avoid scalding themselves with hot food.

[China] Fang Yuan, female, teacher

我挺喜欢用筷子的。因为我觉得很有意思，对我来说这是一种吃饭的新方法。我家乡的朋友知道我学会了用筷子，觉得是一件了不起的事情，因为我们习惯了用手吃饭。我觉得用筷子吃饭的另一个好处就是对身体很好，可以让手指变得很灵活。

[也门] 那比尔，男，大学生

I'm fond of using chopsticks. Because I think it is very interesting and it's a new way of eating. When my friends back in my hometown came to know that I have learnt to use chopsticks, they all regarded this as a great thing, because we are accustomed to eating with our hands. Another advantage I found about eating with chopsticks is that it is beneficial to our health and can make our fingers very flexible.

[Republic of Yemen] Nabil, male, college student

小链接 ADDITIONAL INFORMATION

筷子舞表演
Chopstick dance

筷子舞是蒙古族的一种民间舞蹈，因用筷子伴舞而得名，一般在举办婚礼或喜庆宴会时表演。表演时，舞者两手各握一把扎着红绸的筷子，在众人的歌声和音乐的伴奏下，用筷子击打手、臂、肩、背、腰、腿、脚等身体各个部位，时而也用筷子击打地面。姿态有跪、坐、立等，边打边舞，节奏感和表现力都很强，现已成为舞台上经常上演的节目。

As a Mongolian folk dance, the chopstick dance derived its name from the chopsticks used as props while dancing and is generally performed on such occasions as weddings or festive banquets. While performing, the dancer holds a bunch of chopsticks tied with red silks respectively in each hand. Accompanied by people's singing and music, the dancer beats every part of his body including the palms, arms, shoulder, back, waist, legs, feet and so on, meanwhile, he would also occasionally hit the ground with chopsticks. Dancing postures include kneeling, sitting, standing and so forth, which are integrated with continuous beating. Its regular movements and strong expressive power made the dance a popular performance on various stages.

问候礼节
Greeting Etiquette

导入 INTRODUCTION

　　中国人见面打招呼，熟人之间常嘘寒问暖。比如晨练时相遇，会说"今天天气真冷啊"或"今天天儿真好"之类的话。在午饭或晚饭时相遇，会问"吃了吗？"如果在其他时间相遇，则会根据不同情境，用"出去啊"、"下班了"、"回来了"等问候语来打招呼。而与关系一般或初次相识的朋友见面时，彼此会客气地说"你好"，与长者打招呼则用"您好"。

When meeting their acquaintances, Chinese people usually greet each other by inquiring about one's well-being. For instance, people will say things like "今天天气真冷啊" (What a cold day!) or "今天天儿真好" (What a fine day!) when they encounter together during morning exercises. At lunch time or dinner, they may ask "吃了吗？" (Have you eaten?) If they meet at other times, they may adjust their greetings according to specific circumstances and say things like "出去啊" (Will you go out?), "下班了" (Have you come off duty?), "回来了" (Oh, you are back), etc. However, when encountering ordinary friends or someone they've just met for the first time, people tend to show their politeness by saying "你好" (hello) to their peers or "您好" (a more respectful form of hello) to the elders.

　　问候礼节是每个国家历史文化传统的重要组成部分，中国古代的问候礼节复杂繁琐，主要有磕头跪拜礼、作揖礼和鞠躬礼等。

　　磕头跪拜主要用于庄严隆重的场合，是官员觐见皇帝，家族成员祭祖、敬神或农历新年晚辈向长辈拜年时所行的大礼，体现了中国传统文化对尊卑长幼秩序的重视以及对祖先、

Greeting etiquette is an essential component of the historical and cultural traditions of every country. Greeting etiquette in ancient China was very elaborate and complicated, including mainly kowtow, *zuoyi* (making a bow with hands folded in front) and bowing.

Mainly found on solemn occasions, kowtow is a formal etiquette conducted by officials meeting emperors, family members worshipping their ancestors and gods, or

跪拜俑
A pottery figurine in kowtow position

神灵的情感和态度。

作揖是古代中国人最常用、最简便的问候方式，方法是：两手抱拳，身体略向前弯，以此向人敬礼。随着时代和社会生活的发展，如今跪拜礼和作揖礼都不再是中国人普遍使用的问候方式了，跪拜礼仅在祭祀时使用，作揖礼则成为学习武术的人们相互之间问候的礼仪。

鞠躬也是一种在古代就有的问候礼仪。鞠躬的含义有两个：一是弯身行礼；二是小心谨慎的样子。三国时期蜀相诸葛亮"鞠躬尽瘁，死而后已"的故事在中国家喻户晓。后世常用"鞠躬尽瘁"来赞扬那些谨慎而忘我地工作，为国家或民族事业贡献出全部精力的人。在当代中国，鞠躬礼是一种在正式场合，如婚礼中

作揖雕塑
Sculpture featuring zuoyi

juniors offering lunar New Year greetings to their elders. This etiquette reflects a traditional Chinese cultural emphasis on the power distance between superordinates and subordinates, as well as between seniors and juniors; besides, it also reveals the sentiment and attitude towards ancestors and gods in traditional Chinese culture.

Zuoyi is the most common and easiest greeting method used by ancient people. To perform this etiquette, one first folds his hands in front, and then bends the upper part of his body slightly forward so as to express respect for others. With the development of the times and social life, kowtow and *zuoyi* are no longer commonly used by Chinese people as ways of greeting. The former is restricted to worship while the latter became a greeting method among martial arts learners.

The bow ("鞠躬" in Chinese) is also a greeting method existing since ancient times. This etiquette has two meanings: the first one is bending to show respect; the second one is demonstration of carefulness and caution. The story of Zhuge Liang (Prime Minister of the Shu State in the Three Kingdoms Period)

新人互拜、迎接宾客或向逝者表达哀思时使用的礼节。

婚礼中相互鞠躬的新人
A bride and groom bowing to each other at a wedding

在中国人的日常生活中，还有一些简便易行的礼节，如喝茶时的致谢礼。在主人为客人倒茶或宴席上邻座的朋友为你续茶时，除了说"谢谢"以外，你还可以用食指和中指轻敲桌面，以表示感谢。

握手是现代国际交往及当代中国人最普遍的问候礼节，多用于见面和告别时。有时向别人表示感谢、慰问、祝贺或和解，也使用握手礼。握手是一种无声的语言，也是人与人之间表达态度和情感的一种方式。握手的顺序一般是主人、长辈、上级、女士先主动伸出手，客人、晚辈、下属、男士再相迎握手。当一方先伸出手时，另一方应毫不迟疑地回握，同

who "鞠躬尽瘁，死而后已" (worked so hard for the state until his death) is known to every Chinese person. Later, the expression "鞠躬尽瘁" was used to praise those people who devote all their time and energy to state or national causes. In contemporary China, the bow is a formal etiquette employed by people on formal occasions, such as couples greeting each other at weddings, hosts welcoming guest, or mourners expressing grief regarding the deceased.

In Chinese people's daily life, there are some other simple etiquette, such as expressing gratitude when drinking tea. When a host pours tea for the guests or a friend sitting next to you adds tea for you, apart from saying "谢谢" (thank you), you can also tap the table with the index and middle fingers to extend your gratitude.

The handshake is the most common used greeting etiquette in modern international communications and contemporary China. It is mostly employed when meeting and bidding farewell to people. Sometimes it can even be applied to express gratitude, concern and congratulations, or make reconciliations. As a silent language, handshaking also acts as a way of conveying attitudes and emotions among people. Generally, the host, elders, superiors and ladies will stretch out their hands first, and then the guests, juniors, subordinates and gentlemen will shake their hands. As one party stretches out his/her hand, the other should not hesitate to hold back, and meanwhile should pay attention to the strength of holding, posture and duration.

时还应注意握手的力度、姿势与时间的长短。在中国，家人、朋友与熟人之间很少使用握手礼，在家庭聚会或一般的社交场合，中国人也很少使用西方人习以为常的拥抱礼与吻面礼。

握手礼
Handshaking

In China, family members, friends and acquaintances rarely shake hands with each other. Furthermore, at family gatherings or ordinary social events, nor do they hug or kiss as westerners may be accustomed to.

三言两语
A FEW REMARKS

我常常带着女儿参加一些朋友的聚会，借助这种场合对她进行礼仪教育。开始的时候她并不习惯，但只要她做得好，我会马上表扬她。女儿在这种肯定中，越来越通情达礼。中国是礼仪之邦，我认为这方面的教育对孩子来说是非常重要的。

[中国] 崔成伟，男，国家公务员

I often take my daughter to my friends' party to teach her some social etiquette. At the beginning when she was not accustomed to it, I would praise her as long as she did well. Under this kind of confirmation, my daughter gradually developed a good sense. China is known as a country of courtesy, that's why I regard such education as extremely important for children.
[China] Cui Chengwei , male, national civil servant

有时候看国外的电影和电视剧，孩子直呼长辈的名字，我就觉得有些别扭，当然这可能是出于人人平等的原因吧。按照中国的礼仪传统，直呼长辈姓名是不尊重对方的表现。我有几个朋友允许孩子直呼自己的姓名，觉得这样的家庭氛围很宽松、民主。但我不是很能接受这一点，我觉得称谓是血脉延续的象征，至少在正式场合不能直呼长辈姓名。

[中国] 周晓燕，女，银行职员

Sometimes when I hear children in foreign movies and TV series addressing their elders directly by their first names, I feel uncomfortable. They may think that everyone is equal. According to traditional Chinese etiquette, this is a display of disrespect for the elders. Some of my friends allow their children to address them by their names, which they consider can foster a relaxing and democratic family atmosphere. But I cannot accept that. As for me, address terms are the symbols of family inheritance and we should at least avoid addressing our elders directly by their names on formal occasions.

[China] Zhou Xiaoyan, female, bank clerk

中国人和韩国人都喜欢喝酒，但

Both Chinese and Koreans like drinking wine, but the drinking etiquette is not totally the same. Now

喝酒时的礼仪不太一样。现在跟你们谈谈韩国人喝酒的礼仪：相对而坐的人要互相倒酒；对方酒没喝完时不能添酒；面对长辈时要背过身去喝酒；晚辈一般不号召大家举杯；等等。别看从中国到韩国不是很遥远，文化差异还是很明显的。

[韩国] 朴永顺，男，公司职员

I will talk about South Korean drinking etiquette with you. For example, people who sit opposite to each other are supposed to pour wine for each other. You cannot add wine for the other party until he/she finishes their wine. The younger ones are usually not supposed to propose a toast and are expected to turn around to drink when facing with the elders. The cultural differences between China and South Korea are obvious despite their close distance.
[South Korea] Park Yeong Sun, male, company staff

小链接 ADDITIONAL INFORMATION

互相碰鼻是新西兰毛利人特有的见面礼节。当尊贵的客人到来时，毛利人部落中的长者会依照传统向客人致以最高礼节，即双方用鼻尖相互轻碰两次或三次，相碰次数越多，时间越长，说明礼遇越高。毛利人认为碰鼻可以使彼此心意相通，同呼吸共命运，因而碰鼻有相亲相爱和彼此友好的含义。

毛利人的碰鼻礼
Nose-touching of the Maoris

Mutual nose-touching is the meeting etiquette unique to Maoris in New Zealand. Upon the arrival of a distinguished guest, Maori tribal elders would follow the tradition and honor him/her with their highest greeting etiquette—two or three slight touches on each other's nose tips. The more times the touches and the longer time they take, the higher respect the guests receive. Maoris believe touching the noses can link people's minds together and make them breathe in the same fate, hence the implication of mutual love and friendliness.

小学生的一天
One Day of Elementary Students

可爱的小学生，田琨摄
Lovely pupils, photographed by Tian Kun

中国的小学每年有春、秋两个学期。秋季的开学时间在9月初，1月中旬至2月下旬为寒假；春季的开学时间一般在2月底或3月初，7月中旬至8月底是暑假。

In China, one school year of a primary school consists of two semesters: the spring semester and the autumn semester. The latter starts from early September with a winter vacation lasting from mid-January to late February; while the spring semester usually begins at the end of February or the beginning of March and ends with a summer vacation from mid-July to the end of August.

中国在现阶段实施九年义务教育制度，公立学校在小学六年和初中三年的基础教育阶段不收学费。这一制度始于20世纪80年代中期。1986年4月12日，第六届全国人民代表大会第四次会议通过了《中华人民共和国义务教育法》，同年7月1日开始施行。2006年6月29日，第十届全国人民代表大会常务委员会第二十二次会议又

《中华人民共和国义务教育法》
Compulsory Education Law of the People's Republic of China

At its present stage, China implements the nine-year compulsory education system, which means public schools charge no intuition fees during the six years of primary school and three years of middle school education. The system originated in the mid-1980s. On April 12th, 1986, the *Compulsory Education Law of the People's Republic of*

修订通过了新《中华人民共和国义务教育法》，于2006年9月1日起施行。

中国儿童一般在6—7岁时进入小学一年级。每天在学校上7节课，上午4节课，下午3节课，每节大约40分钟。小学高年级学生也有每天上9节课的。主课有数学、语文、英语，副课有体育、美术、音乐、品德、写字、手工、自然、信息技术等。下午放学后，有兴趣爱好或有特长的学生还可以参加学校组织的课外活动，如棒球、足球、机器人比赛和管乐队等等。

新课标小学生语文课本
Chinese textbook for pupils in the New National Curriculum

在北京和上海等大城市，很多学龄孩子从周一到周日都很忙。阳阳是一名家住北京的小学五年级学生。周一至周五，她每天早上7点准时起床，收拾书包，吃早饭。7点40分以前，妈妈陪她走到学校门口。8点以前，孩子们在教室里晨读，8点开始上课。上午的课一般是数学、语文、英语、品德等，下午的课有音乐、体育、美术等。中午阳阳和很多孩子一样在学校用餐、午休。下午4点半放

China was adopted at the 4th Session of the 6th National People's Congress, and came into effect on July 1st the same year. On June 29th, 2006, the law was amended and passed at the 22nd Session of the Standing Committee of the 10th National People's Congress and came into effect on September 1st, 2006.

Chinese children usually enter the first grade at the age of six or seven. They have seven classes every day, four in the morning and three in the afternoon. Each class lasts about 40 minutes. Some students of senior grade even have nine classes each day, ranging from the main subjects such as Math, Chinese and English to the minor subjects such as PE, Art, Music, Morality, Writing, Crafts, Nature, and IT, etc. After school in the afternoon, students who are interested or skilled in certain fields can also participate in extracurricular activities organized by their schools, such as baseball, basketball, robot match and brass band, etc.

In big cities like Beijing and Shanghai, many school-age children are occupied from Monday to Sunday. For example, Yangyang, a fifth-grade student in Beijing, always gets up at seven o'clock in the morning, then packs up her bag, eats breakfast and gets to the school gate accompanied by her mother before 7:40. The children will do morning reading in the classroom until eight o'clock when the class begins. Morning classes are generally Math, Chinese, English and

学。晚饭前后，阳阳要做语文、数学、英语等科目的作业，预习第二天的课程，这些一般在两小时内可以完成。每天她还要在妈妈的督促下练钢琴。阳阳喜欢读课外书，如果有时间，她也会上网玩儿游戏。中国年轻一代的父母非常重视对孩子教育的投入，常常利用双休日给孩子报各种各样的课外辅导班，这使不少孩子感到周末比平时还累。阳阳周末也很忙，除了完成学校的作业外，周六上午她还要参加奥林匹克数学培训班（简称"奥数班"），晚上要参加合唱团预备团员培训班。周日上午上英语辅导班，晚上还有钢琴课。尽管许多家长并不希望孩子上这么多辅导班，但为了"小升初"能考上一所好学校，为了不让孩子输在起跑线上，不得不牺牲孩子的玩耍时间。

美丽的小学校园
A beautiful primary school

Morality, etc., whereas the afternoon classes cover Music, PE, Art and so on. At noon, Yangyang eats lunch and takes a nap at school just as many other children do. Then they leave school at 4:30. Around dinner time, Yangyang has to spend generally no more than 2 hours on her homework concerning subjects such as Chinese, Math and English, and prepare for classes on the next day. Moreover, she has to practice the piano under the supervision of her mother. Yangyang also likes reading extracurricular books and if time is available, she will play online games. The younger generation parents in China attach great importance to their children's education and often register their children for various extracurricular classes on the weekends, and this makes their children even more tired. For Yangyang, she is also busy on the weekends. Apart from the homework assigned at school, she has to take the Olympic Math courses on Saturday mornings and attend a training class in the evenings in order to obtain a choir membership. She has English training classes on Sunday mornings as well as piano lessons in the evenings. Although many parents don't want their children to take so many remedial classes, they have to sacrifice children's playing time to guarantee that their children can be admitted to a good middle school and that they won't fall behind at the starting line.

三言两语 A FEW REMARKS

我们每天语文、数学、外语的家庭作业都是一张A4纸，加上预习、复习和拓展阅读，最多两个小时搞定，学习负担并不算重，但周末会感觉比较累，特别是星期六晚上上奥数班的时候，困了我们就吃两颗很酸、很酸的糖，班里的小朋友都吃，然后就可以精神一会儿……

[中国] 李佳琪，女，小学生

The time spent on our daily homework of Chinese, Math, English written on a piece of A4 paper, together with the time for preparation, review and further reading is no more than 2 hours. That's not a heavy learning task. However, I feel tired on the weekends, especially when I take the Olympic Math courses on Saturday evenings. Every time when we are sleepy, all of our classmates will eat two very, very sour candies to stay energetic for a while…

[China] Li Jiaqi, female, primary school student

现在不光孩子累，我们这些当家长的也累。我家孩子刚上一年级时，认字不多，老师布置的作业记不清，晚上就经常和其他家长通消息，非常累。现在好多了，学校布置些软性作业，用来培养习惯的。第一个月时，我们和孩子一样非常不适应，但慢慢累积经验，能找出一些窍门来，特别是孩子在不断成长，家长前面下的功夫多，后面就可以放手得早一些，所以开始累一点儿还是值得的。

[中国] 王学军，男，记者

Nowadays, not only the children but also we parents are very tired. When my kid was in the first grade, she was too young to learn so many characters and remember the homework assigned by her teacher, so I was forced to talk with other parents which made me very weary. But things are much better now. The school gives them some "soft homework" to cultivate their good habits. During the first month, we felt uncomfortable, but with the accumulation of our experience, some tips could be found. What is important is that my child is growing healthily. The more efforts we parents make earlier, the earlier we can let our children go. It's worthwhile to be tired at the beginning

[China] Wang Xuejun, male, journalist

中国家庭教育孩子的方式和我们德国完全不同，我觉得中国的父母管得太多了。我小时候摔了跤爸爸妈妈都不会扶我起来，哭也没有用，还是得自己爬起来；长大以后学习什么专业爸爸妈妈也不管，他们说你自己感兴趣就行了，哪一行社会都需要。所以我很自立，早就学会了自己做事情，自己进行选择。

[德国] 汉斯，男，研究生

The way that Chinese families educate their children is totally different from that in Germany. I think Chinese parents interfere too much with their children. When I fell down as a kid, my parents didn't help me up. Crying didn't work at all, and I had to get up by myself. They didn't intervene with my major choices and told me I could choose whatever I am interested in, because every profession is needed in the society. Therefore, I am very self-reliant, and have learned to do things by myself and choose what I want.

[Germany] Hans, male, graduate student

据上世纪80年代的资料统计，中国每年有100多万小学生因家庭贫困交不起四五十元的书费、杂费而失学。为了救助贫困地区的失学儿童，让他们完成学业，改善贫困地区的办学条件，中国共青团中央和中国青少年发展基金会于1989年发起一项名为"希望工程"的社会公益事业，并于1990年在安徽省金寨县援建了第一所希望小学。20年后，截至2009年年底，希望工程已累计募集捐款56亿7000多万元人民币，资助家庭经济困难的学生340多万名，在贫困地区建设希望小学15900所，培训农村小学教师52000余名，为缩小中国教育的地域差别，促进贫困地区基础教育事业的发展作出了重要贡献。

According to statistics of the 1980s, over one million primary school students in China dropped out of school because they couldn't afford the 40 to 50 RMB fees on books and other items. To help children who dropped out of school in poverty-stricken areas to complete their studies and improve their school conditions, the Central Committee of the Chinese Communist Youth League and the China Youth Development Foundation initiated a social welfare undertaking called Project Hope in 1989. Afterwards in 1990, the first primary school sponsored by the project was founded in Jinzhai County, Anhui Province. Twenty years later, by the end of 2009, Project Hope had raised over 5.67 billion RMB, aiding more than 3.4 million financially disadvantaged students, building over 15,900 primary schools in poor areas, training over 52,000 primary school teachers in rural areas, and this has made great contribution to the reduction of regional educational differences and the promotion of development of rudimentary education in poor areas.

希望工程图标
The logo of the Project Hope

Chinese Culture Symbols

文化符号

印刷术
Printing

2008年北京奥运会开幕式上活字印刷术展示
Typography shown in the opening ceremony of 2008 Beijing Olympic Games

在2008年北京奥运会开幕式上，活版印刷术的展示极其壮观：孔子的三千弟子手持竹简吟诵着《论语》步入场内，场地中间出现了此起彼伏的"活字"，而后不同时代的"和"字跃然而出，表达了孔子"以和为贵"的人文理念，彰显了中华民族的和谐观。

In the opening ceremony of the Beijing Olympic Games in 2008, typography was demonstrated in a spectacular way in which the Confucius's three thousand disciples stepped in holding bamboo slips while reciting *The Analects of Confucius*. Movable types rose one after another in the middle of the stage and the Chinese character "和" (harmony) from different ages appeared vividly before people's eyes, expressing Confucius's humanistic idea that "peace is the most precious" while also revealing the Chinese nation's view regarding harmony.

印刷术发明之前文化的传播主要靠手抄书籍，既费时又费力，还容易出现错误。在印章和石刻的启示下，隋朝时发明了雕版印刷，宋代毕升又发明了活版印刷。中国的印刷术是人类近代文明的先导，为知识的广泛传播创造了条件。印刷术首先传到亚洲和欧洲，而后在世

Before the invention of printing, culture was mainly transmitted via handwritten books which are not only time-consuming and energy-consuming but were also error prone. Inspired by seals and stone inscriptions, people in the Sui Dynasty invented block printing and then Bi Sheng in the Song Dynasty invented typography. China's printing is the forerunner of modern civilization

年画雕版
A cut block for printing New Year pictures

界范围内普及开来。

　　隋炀帝（569—618）时创建了
科举制度，用写文章的办法选拔官
员，传播好文章的要求在社会上出现
了。专业抄书匠们为了大量复制好文
章，仿照拓片技术进行复印，而后又
结合印章阳文反书法发明了雕版印刷
术。其出现的年代大约在盛唐至中唐
之间，盛行于北宋，最后由毕升发明
了活版印刷。活版印刷是印刷史上一
次伟大的技术革命，方法是先制成单
字的阳文反文字模，然后按照稿件把单字挑选出来排列在字盘内涂墨

铅活字字模
Movable types made of lead

and created the conditions for wide-spread knowledge. Printing was first introduced to other Asian countries and Europe and then spread throughout the world.

As Emperor Yang of the Sui Dynasty created an imperial examination system to select officials based on their articles, the need for transmitting good articles appeared in society. Aiming at massive replication of good articles, professional book copyists duplicated the articles by imitating the technique of rubbing and then invented block printing by borrowing the technique of making reversed and raised words on seals. Block printing emerged between the prime time of the Tang Dynasty and the middle Tang Dynasty and prevailed in the Song Dynasty. At last, Bi Sheng invented typography which brought about a great technological revolution. Typography entails making a type matrix with inversed and raised individual characters and then by putting ink in the case in which individual characters picked out according to the manuscript are placed in the order needed for printing. After that, the type matrix is taken out for typesetting and printing next time.

Printing originated in China and printing of many countries was introduced from China or developed under the influence of Chinese printing. Japan, the first to be

古登堡像
Picture of Gutenberg

印刷，印完后再将字模拆出留待下次排印时使用。

中国是印刷术的发明地，很多国家的印刷术或是由中国传入，或是在中国印刷术的影响下发展起来的。日本便是最早受到影响的一个，公元8世纪就可以用雕版印佛经了。朝鲜10世纪也开始用雕版印制佛经。中国的雕版印刷技术大约在14世纪由波斯传到埃及。波斯实际上成了中国印刷技术西传的中转站，14世纪末欧洲才出现雕版印制的纸牌、圣像和拉丁文课本。

中国发明的活版印刷在欧洲得到了进一步完善，德国人谷登堡在1440—1448年间创造的铅合金活字版印刷术被世界各国广泛应用，奠定了现代印刷术的基础。1845年德

influenced by Chinese printing, began to print Buddhist scriptures with block printing from the 8th century and then North Korea did so too starting in the 10th century. The block printing technology in China was passed from Persia to Egypt around the 14th century. Persia, in fact, became the transfer station for the spread of printing technology to the West. It was at the end of the 14th century that playing cards, icons, and Latin textbooks appeared in Europe.

Typography invented in China was further improved in Europe. Mechanical typography with types of lead metal alloy, which was invented by Gutenberg of Germany from 1440 to 1448, was widely spread all over the world and laid a foundation for modern printing. After the first rapid printer appeared in Germany in 1845, the mechanization of printing technology began.

Since the 1950s, printing technology developed to modernization by constantly adopting the achievements in emerging science and technology such as electronic technology, laser technology, information technology and polymer chemistry. With the great progress of modern science and technology, printing technology has also changed a lot. The sea of books that we see in libraries today must be attributed to the invention and improvement of printing.

国生产了第一台快速印刷机，开始了印刷技术的机械化过程。

从20世纪50年代开始，印刷技术不断地采用电子技术、激光技术、信息科学以及高分子化学等新兴科学技术所取得的成果，进入了现代化的发展阶段。随着近代科学技术的飞跃发展，印刷技术也迅速改变着面貌。今天我们可以在图书馆看到浩如烟海的书籍，必须归功于印刷术的发明与完善。

清华大学图书馆，田琨摄
The library in Tsinghua University, photographed by Tian Kun

三言两语 A FEW REMARKS

做排字工并不难，要的就是熟练。我二十岁时到天津师范大学印刷厂上班，开始做排字工作。我绝没有想到铅字印刷竟会有被淘汰的命运，至今觉得铅字印的书报看得特别清楚。其实铅字印刷和激光照排出来的书报没什么区别，我之所以有那样的感觉，是因为干排字工年头多了，和这些小小的铅字感情太深的缘故。

[中国] 李秀琪，女，退休工人

我至今对2008年北京奥运会开幕式上展示的活字印刷术记忆犹新，印刷术是中国的四大发明之一，这我上小学的时候就知道，因为老师在历史课上讲过。可对于我来说，印刷术仅仅是一个课本上的概念，完全没有感性认识。自从看了北京奥运会开幕式上的展示，我才真正惊叹它的伟大。

[泰国] 林美芳，女，中学教师

The job of typesetting is not difficult but requires proficiency. At the age of 20, I took the job of typesetting in a printing house in Tianjin Normal University. It never occurred to me that type printing may fall into disuse one day and I still feel that the words in books and newspapers of type printing are quite distinct. In fact, books and newspapers made by type printing and by laser typesetting do not have many differences. I feel so because I work as a typesetter for such a long time that I have deep affection for the small types.

[China] Li Xiuqi, female, retired worker

I still have a fresh memory of the typography shown in the opening ceremony of the Beijing Olympic Games in 2008. Printing is among the four great inventions of ancient China, which I have known since the teacher told us in a history course in primary school. For me, however, printing was only a concept in textbooks and I had no perceptual knowledge about it. It was not until the demonstration of typography in the opening ceremony of the Beijing Olympic Games that I was really amazed by its greatness.

[Thailand] Lin Meifang, female, middle school teacher

在现代汉字印刷技术方面，北京大学教授王选（1937—2006）作出了突出贡献。1975年5月王选开始主持照排系统研制工作，1979年7月27日，在北京大学的计算机房里，科研人员用自己研制的照排系统一次成版输出了一张由各种大小字体组成、版面布局复杂的八开报纸样纸，报头是"汉字信息处理"六个大字。这是首次用激光照排机输出的中文报纸版面，这项成果为世界上最浩繁的文字——汉字告别铅字印刷开辟了通畅的大道，对实现中国新闻出版印刷领域的现代化具有重大意义，被誉为中国印刷技术的再次革命。

Wang Xuan (1937-2006), a professor of Peking University, made a great contribution to modern Chinese printing technology. In May 1975, Wang Xuan began to take charge of developing the photo-typesetting system. On July 27th, 1979, researchers used their own photo-typesetting system to type out an octavo sample of newspaper with various font sizes and complex layouts for the first time in the computer room in Peking University. The masthead of the newspaper was "汉字信息处理" (Chinese character information processing). This was the first Chinese newspaper typed out with the laser photo-typesetting system. This achievement was reputed as a new revolution in Chinese printing technology for it paved an unobstructed way for leaving off type printing for printing Chinese, the language with vast and numerous characters in the world, and has held great significance in modernizing Chinese news publishing and printing.

王选教授（右）在《财富》论坛上和同行交流
Professor Wang Xuan (at right) was communicating with his peer at the Fortune Forum.

灯 笼
Lantern

导入 INTRODUCTION

　　前门大街是北京著名的商业街，位于北京中轴线上，发源于明代。明代北京突破了元代"前朝后市"的定制，在正阳门（前门的正式名称）一带形成了大商业区，清朝又出现了作坊、茶楼和戏园，后来京奉铁路、京汉铁路开通，在前门设立了东西两个火车站，前门商业盛极一时。从古至今，这条商业街上都是大红灯笼高高挂。

前门大街上的大红灯笼，田琨摄
The red lanterns in Qianmen Street, photographed by Tian Kun

The famous business street—Qianmen Street in Beijing is located along the city's central axis and originated in the Ming Dynasty. In the Ming Dynasty, Beijing broke the rule of "placing the imperial court in front of the palace and the market behind the palace" and a large business district was formed surrounding Zhengyangmen (the official name of Qianmen). In the Qing Dynasty, workshops, tea houses and theaters appeared and two railway stations were established to the east and west of Qianmen after the opening of the Jing-Feng Railway and Jing-Han Railway. During that time, business in Qianmen district saw its best days. In all ages, red lanterns have hung high along this business street.

　　中国的灯笼统称为灯彩，起源于西汉（前206—公元25），每年农历正月十五元宵节人们都挂起象征团圆与红火的大红灯笼来营造一种喜庆的气氛。灯笼集绘画、剪纸、纸扎、刺缝等工艺于一体，种类有宫灯、纱

Chinese lanterns, collectively known as *dengcai* (colored lanterns), originated in the Western Han Dynasty (206 BC-AD 25). On lunar January 15th of each year, people will hang red lanterns symbolizing reunion and prosperity to create a joyous atmosphere. Combining painting, paper cutting, paper

前门大街的"盛世"走马灯，田琨摄

The trotting horse lantern named Flourishing Age in Qianmen Street, photographed by Tian Kun

灯、吊灯、走马灯等，造型多种多样，除常规的圆形、方形外还有人物、山水、花鸟、龙凤、鱼虫等形状。

灯笼与中国人的生活息息相关，从古至今，庙宇中、大街上、庭院里，处处都可以看到灯笼。中国的灯笼不仅用以照明，往往还是一种象征。台湾灯艺大师吴敦厚说，人们结婚时会请他做新娘灯，代表着喜庆。更有意思的是，因"灯"与"丁"语音相近，还意味着人丁兴旺。

尽管一年到头人们都能看见灯笼，但最让人企盼的还是元宵节的花灯。元宵观灯的习俗起源于西汉

挂着大红灯笼的路灯，田琨摄

The street lamp on which red lanterns hang, photographed by Tian Kun

pasting and embroidery, lanterns have various types such as palace lanterns, gauze lanterns, pendant lanterns and trotting horse lanterns as well as various shapes including not only commonly seen round and square shapes but also shapes of human figures, landscapes, flowers, birds, dragons, phoenixes, fish and insects.

Lanterns are so closely associated with daily life that they are seen everywhere such as in temples, streets and yards in all ages. Chinese lanterns are not only used for illumination but also as a symbol. The master of lantern art in Taiwan, Wu Dunhou, said that he was invited to make bride lanterns for weddings to symbolize happiness and celebration. What is more interesting is that "deng", the Chinese pronunciation of lantern, also represents a large number of family members for "deng" has a similar pronunciation with "ding" (meaning the number of family members).

Although lanterns can be seen all around the year, people look forward to the festive lanterns of the Lantern Festival most. The custom of viewing the lanterns during the Lantern Festival originated in the beginning of the Western Han Dynasty and prevailed in the Tang Dynasty. The Kaiyuan

初年，至唐大盛，开元年间为庆祝国泰民安大制花灯，以闪烁的灯光象征"彩龙兆祥，民富国强"。明朱元璋建都南京时，更是于秦淮河上燃放万

元宵节花灯
Festive lanterns in the Lantern Festival

支水灯，有如天上银河般灿烂。如今是一个文化多元化的时代，各种文化的交流日益频繁，灯笼已成为一种独特的中国文化符号为世界各国人民所知，而且融入了许多现代元素，在传统的基础上更加发扬光大，形状越来越繁多，颜色越来越艳丽，就像我们今天的生活。

灯笼除了照明以外，还有其他的意义。过去每年正月私塾①开学时，家长会为子女准备一盏灯笼，由老师点亮，象征学生的前途一片光明，称为"开灯"。后来由此演变成元宵节提灯笼的习俗，有时还特意在灯笼上绘制历史故事与民间传说，以教导子孙后代认识自己的文化，所以灯笼还

period in the Tang Dynasty witnessed the mass production of festive lanterns to celebrate peace and prosperity for the blinking lights holding the meaning that colored dragons were propitious signs indicating a prosperous nation and powerful people. When Emperor Hongwu made Nanjing the capital of the Ming Dynasty, he required people to light and set afloat thousands of water lanterns that were as bright as the Milky Way. In today's era featuring cultural diversity and frequent cultural communication, lanterns became known as a symbol of Chinese culture all over the world. They also absorbed some modern elements and developed to a higher stage on the basis of tradition. With their increasing number of shapes and growingly bright and beautiful colors, they embody the feel just like our life today.

The significance of lanterns is not limited to illumination. In the past, when *sishu*① was opened every lunar January, parents would prepare their children a lantern to be lit by the teacher, the act which is called *kai deng* (light the lantern), symbolizing the bright future of students. Later, this custom evolved into carrying the lantern around during the Lantern Festival. Sometimes people may specially draw pictures of historical stories and folk legends on the lanterns to teach later generations about their own culture. Therefore, lanterns can also be used to pass on national culture from generation to generation.

Despite the modern lighting equipment

①私塾：中国古代开设于家庭、宗族或乡村内部的民间幼儿教育机构，即私立学校，教育内容以儒家思想为中心。

① *Sishu* refers to private early childhood education institution established inside homes, clans and villages in ancient China. It is also known as private school. The education focuses on Confucianism.

具有薪火相传的作用。

在照明设备已十分现代化的今天，古老的灯笼仍然有着独特的魅力，且不说参照古代灯笼设计的现代灯具，就是原汁原味的古代灯笼也时常会高悬于现代化的建筑之上或道路两旁，依然给我们带来别具一格的喜庆与祥和的气氛，具有浓郁的传统文化韵味。

大红灯笼高高挂，田琨摄
The red lanterns hang high, photographed by Tian Kun

today, the old lanterns still maintain their special charm. Some modern lamps imitate the design of ancient lanterns. What is more, even lanterns with antique taste were often hung high on modern buildings or on both sides of roads, bringing us a distinct festive and peaceful atmosphere through its strong flavoring with traditional culture.

在发明电灯之前，灯笼是一种灯具，现在灯笼就只是一种装饰性物品了。每年的春节到十五，我们家都会挂起红灯笼，象征团团圆圆、红红火火，营造出一种喜庆的气氛，让人心情特别愉悦。

[中国] 楚亚飞，男，大学生

我已经有二三十年不扎花灯了，我祖上是扬州北乡的，爷爷扎得一手好灯，我十多岁的时候就跟他学扎灯手艺，一直扎到1992年太平寺巷拆迁。现在扎花灯的人少了，老早住平房时，一进几大间，家中的房梁上、阁楼上都挂满了龙凤灯、荷花灯等各式各样的灯，可好看呢！

[中国] 陆庭荣，男，花灯手艺人

Lanterns were used for illumination before the invention of the electric lamp but are used for decoration today. From the Spring Festival to the Lantern Festival every year, we hang red lanterns in our family dwellings as a symbol of reunion and prosperity. They create a festive atmosphere and delight us a lot.

[China] Chu Yafei, male, university student

I have not made festive lanterns for about twenty or thirty years. My family root was in Beixiang Town of Yangzhou City. My grandfather used to be an expert in making festive lanterns. I learned the technique from him when I was about 10 years old and did not stop making lanterns until 1992 when the Taiping Temple Lane was removed. Today, only a few people make festive lanterns. When I lived in the bungalow a long time ago, there were many rooms in the house and the beautiful lanterns of various shapes such as dragon-phoenix lanterns and lotus-shaped lanterns were hung all over on the beams and in the lofts.

[China] Lu Tingrong, male, festive lantern maker

我觉得中国的灯笼很漂亮，鲜艳的颜色很抢眼，你想不看都不行。希腊人很喜欢蓝色和白色，看看我们的国旗，看看我们的大海和房屋就知道了。我经常想中国人为什么喜欢红色，我觉得首先和大自然有关系，因为太阳是红的，最漂亮的花也是红的。

[希腊] 艾丽丝，女，大学生

I think that Chinese lanterns are quite beautiful. Their bright colors are so eye-catching that you cannot even ignore them. Greeks love blue and white very much, which can be told by our national flag, our sea and our house. I always wonder why Chinese people love red. I guess that first it is related to nature because the sun is red and the most beautiful flowers are also red.

[Greece] Alice, female, university student

小链接 ADDITIONAL INFORMATION

蓝色港湾是北京著名的国际商区，每到夜晚，这里都亮起璀璨的灯，一年一度的蓝色港湾灯光节更是给大家带来了惊喜和温暖。2012年12月14日，以"缤纷城堡，全城欢庆"为主题的蓝色港湾第五届灯光节开幕，近千人云集中央广场，见证了这个美妙的时刻。此次灯光节有13万平米的灯光秀，如冬季里绽放的郁金香花海、12星座组成的魔幻星空，此外还有蘑菇群、时光隧道、未来世界……充满创意的灯光景观驱走了冬日的寒冷，平添了诸多喜气与热闹。

北京国际商区蓝色港湾的灯笼，田琨摄
The lanterns in Solana, the international business district in Beijing, photographed by Tian Kun

Solana is a famous international business district in Beijing. Bright lamps light up here every night. Not to mention the surprise and warmth brought by the annual Solana Lights Festival. On December 14th in 2012, the 5th Solana Lights Festival was opened with the theme of "castle of multi colors and city in festive celebration". Nearly a thousand people gathered in the central square and experienced the wonderful moment. The Solana Lights Festival of that time had a light show encompassing an area of 130 thousand square meters, including "the sea of tulips blossoming in winter", "the magical starry sky constituting twelve constellations", "mushroom families", "a time tunnel", and "the future world". The creative light show drove away coldness and brought happiness and excitement.

Tourism Highlights
名胜古迹

长　城
The Great Wall

　　长城蜿蜒万里，东端是山海关，西端是嘉峪关。山海关临渤海，位于河北省秦皇岛市东北15公里处，有"天下第一关"之称，四座主要城门与多种防御建筑巍然而立。嘉峪关在嘉峪山上，位于甘肃省嘉峪关市西面5公里处，是古代丝绸之路的交通要冲，由内城、外城、城壕三道防线构成重叠并守之势。山海关与嘉峪关遥相呼应，与其间数不清的关隘共同托起了万里长城。

Meandering for tens of thousands of miles, the Great Wall begins in the east at Shanhaiguan Pass and ends at Jiayuguan Pass in the west. Facing the Bohai Sea, Shanhaiguan Pass is situated 15 kilometers northeast of Qinhuangdao City in Hebei Province, and is regarded as "the number one pass in the world". Its four main gates, together with various kinds of defensive structures, stand in majestic splendor. Jiayuguan Pass lies on Jiayu Mountain 5 kilometers west of Jiayuguan City in Gansu Province. It once served as a transport hub for the ancient Silk Road. Its three lines of defense, including the inner city, outer city and city moat, form an overlapping fortification system. Echoing each other at great distance, Shanhaiguan Pass and Jiayuguan Pass collaboratively form the "ten-thousand *li* Great Wall" with the numerous passes embedded in between.

山海关与嘉峪关
Shanhaiguan Pass and Jiayuguan Pass

长城是中国古代在不同时期为抵御塞北游牧部落联盟侵袭而修筑的规模浩大的军事工程，东西绵延上万华里，因此被称为"万里长城"。长城始建于春秋战国时代，现存的长城遗址主要为14世纪的明长城。国家文物局2009年公布：中国明长城总长度为8851.8千米。长城是中国古代劳动人民创造的伟大的奇迹，是中国悠久历史的见证。

长城
The Great Wall

春秋战国时期，各国诸侯为了防御别国入侵修筑烽火台，并用城墙将诸多烽火台连接起来，形成了最早的长城。此后历代君王几乎都加固增修长城。 据记载，秦始皇使用了近百万劳动力修筑长城，占全国总人口的二十分之一。当时没有任何机械设备，一切都由人力完

The Great Wall is a massive military project that was built in different periods of ancient China to prevent intrusions by allies of nomadic tribes in the north. Stretching for tens of thousands of *li* from east to west, the ancient fortification derived its name the "ten-thousand *li* Great Wall". Construction of the Great Wall started in the Spring and Autumn and the Warring States periods. The majority of the existing walls belong to the 14th century Ming Dynasty walls. According to the announcement made by the State Administration of Cultural Heritage, the Ming Dynasty Great Wall measures 8,851.8 km. As a great wonder created by ancient Chinese people, the Great Wall witnessed the long history of China.

In the Spring and Autumn and the Warring States periods, in order to prevent external invasions, rulers of each state constructed beacon towers and connected them by walls, resulting in the earliest form of the Great Wall. Almost all the subsequent rulers had reinforced or extended the Great Wall. According to the records, the First Emperor of Qin exploited almost one million laborers in the construction of the Great Wall, making up one twentieth of the Qin Dynasty's population. The construction was an arduous task, for no machines existed then, and all work was finished by laborers working in an environment full of high mountains and lofty

成，工作环境又是崇山峻岭，十分
艰难。当时的人恐怕绝没有想到，
这长城一修就是数千年、上万里，
难怪无论古今中外，凡是到过长城
的人都会惊叹它宏伟的规模、磅礴
的气势，长城也因此成为文学艺术
永恒的主题。

日本北陆大学孔子学院墙上的长城挂毯，刘谦功摄

Tapestry of the Great Wall hanging on a wall of the Confucius Institute at Hokuriku University, Japan, photographed by Liu Qiangong

　　居庸关位于北京，有"天下
第一雄关"之称，这里两山对峙，
一水中流，山上城墙蜿蜒，山下城
楼巍峨。关城内庙宇、署馆、亭
坊、仓房层叠错落，红墙、碧瓦、
彩画相映生辉。关城以险峻著称，
有"一夫当关，万夫莫开"之势。
居庸关不仅地势险要，而且风景宜
人。历代文人墨客在此留下了许多
赞咏的诗篇，乾隆皇帝也在此御笔
亲提"居庸叠翠"四字，成为著名

hills. People living in that period probably had never anticipated that the construction of the wall was to last for thousands of years and reach thousands of miles. It is no wonder that people who have been to the Great Wall, regardless of the time and their nationalities, will invariably be impressed by its massive scale and majesty. Therefore, the Great Wall came to establish itself as an eternal theme in literature and art.

Located in Beijing, Juyongguan Pass is referred to as "the most majestic pass in the world". Here, two mountains stand facing each other with a river flowing in between. The top of the mountain is lined with meandering walls, and the mountain foot is full of city towers soaring up to the sky. Inside the city at Juyongguan Pass, temples, office bureaus, pavilions and storehouses are scattered around; the red walls, glazed tiles and colorful paintings set each other off to form a brilliant scene. The exterior of the city is renowned for its precipitousness characterized by the saying "one man guarding the pass will prevent 10,000 enemies from getting through". Juyongguan Pass not only has a terrain of great strategic importance, but also possesses pleasant scenery. Generations of literati and poets had left behind numerous poems praising the natural beauty of the site. The inscriptions of Emperor Qianlong's words "居庸叠翠" (the lush green at Juyongguan Pass) helped it to become one of the famous "eight scenic spots in Beijing".

居庸关
Juyongguan Pass

Rising up in Shanxi Province, Yanmenguan Pass is sided by Yanmen Mountain in the east and Longshan Mountain in the west. Wild geese migrate back and forth between northern and southern China via Yanmenguan Pass, hence the name Yanmenguan (wild geese gate). With a perimeter of one kilometer, the city at Yanmenguan Pass is fortified by walls measuring six meters high and it contains three gates. A tower called Yanlou (wild geese tower) was constructed on the wall above the east gate, with a plaque bearing the word "天险" (natural barrier). The west gate fortress is a temple accommodating the Shrine of Yang Yanzhao (a military general in the Song Dynasty), with a plaque bearing "地利"

的"燕山八景"之一。

雁门关位于山西，东有雁门山，西靠隆山，每年大雁于其间南来北往，故称雁门。雁门关关城周长二

雁门关关楼
Tower above the gate of Yanmenguan Pass

里，墙高一丈八尺，有三座门。东门之上筑有楼台，名曰雁楼，有"天险"石匾；西门之上筑有杨六郎庙，有"地利"石匾。北门未建楼台，门额上书"雁门关"三个大字，左右有对联一副："三关冲要无双地，九寨尊崇第一关。"

长城的伟大与壮观有目共睹，世人皆知，它永远是中华民族的骄傲。

(topographical advantages). No towers were constructed on the north gate, instead three bold characters "雁门关" (Yanmenguan Pass) are inscribed on the lintel of the gate. On the left and right sides of the gate, there is a couplet saying "三关冲要无双地，九寨尊崇第一关" (No place matches Yanmenguan Pass in importance, the pass is honored as the top among all the nine passes).

The grandeur and magnificence of the Great Wall is universally acknowledged and recognized. It will always be the pride of Chinese people.

三言两语 A FEW REMARKS

我是初春去的长城，那时树还没有长满叶子，远处看上去更有一种沧桑感。长城，从当初作为抵御外敌的工事到现在成为中华民族的象征，已经屹立了数千年。它像一条巨龙盘卧在山体之间：山有多高，城有多高；山有多陡，城有多陡。长城太伟大了，我不得不感叹中国古人的智慧与毅力。

[中国] 杨鹏，男，大学生

I visited the Great Wall in early spring when the trees are not yet covered with leaves yet. Viewing from a distance, I felt a sense of vicissitudes. As the fortification against invaders, the Great Wall has been standing for thousands of years and has become a symbol of the Chinese nation in this day. It is crouching on the mountains like a giant dragon. However tall and steep the mountain is, the Great Wall would always conform in the same manner. The Great Wall is so great! I have to say that I am astonished by the wisdom and perseverance of the ancient Chinese people.

[China] Yang Peng, male, college student

我已经去过长城好几次了，有时候自己去玩儿，有时候带朋友去游览，但是我每一次去时还是会有很特别的感觉，因为在长城上我会感到它几千年的历史，而且我特别喜欢站在长城上看风景。我认为长城最能代表中国，是一个非常伟大的工程。

[芬兰] 斯特兰，女，大学生

I've visited the Great Wall several times. Sometimes I have gone there alone, and sometimes I show my friends around there. However, I get a new kind of special feeling every time I visited there. Standing on the Great Wall, I come to experience its history of thousands of years. In particular, I love watching the scenery from the height of the Great Wall. I think the Great Wall best represents China, and it's a very great work.

[Finland] Stellan, female, college student

小链接 ADDITIONAL INFORMATION

　　像中国的万里长城一样，荷兰的拦海大坝也是一项伟大的人造工程。荷兰的须德海原是一个深入内陆的海湾，湾内海岸线长达300公里。1932年筑起了宽90米、高出海平面7米的拦海大坝，此后又不断地把湾内海水抽出，到1982年共造地2600平方公里，剩下的大约一半面积也改造成了一个淡水湖。在这项工程中，荷兰专家设计了开放式方案，在65个高度为30—40米、重量为1.8万吨的坝墩上安装了62个活动钢板闸门，风和日丽时开启，让海水自由来去，风暴来临时便放下去，将汹涌的海水拒之门外。这样既可防洪，也可保护这一带海区的贝壳类动物。如今坝区风景宜人，成为荷兰人休闲的好去处。

荷兰的拦海大坝
The Zuiderzee Works of Netherlands

Same as China's Great Wall, the Netherlands' Zuiderzee Works is also a great manmade project. The Zuiderzee of Netherland was originally an inlet stretching into the inland with a costal line of 300 km. In 1932, a dam measuring 90 meters wide and 7 meters above the sea level was constructed. After that, the water of the inlet was gradually drained, culminating in the 1982 reclamation of 2,600 square meters of land. The remaining half of the inlet was also transformed into a freshwater lake. In this project, the Dutch experts formulated a flexible design, which is to install 62 moveable sluice gates made from steel plates onto 65 dam piers measuring 30-40 meters high and weighing 18,000 tons each. When the weather is fine, the gates are opened, letting the seawater flow freely; when the storm strikes, the gates are closed, preventing the turbulent water from intruding. This can not only control floods, but also protect shellfish in the sea area. The dam area is full of scenic beauty at present day, becoming a desirable resort for people of the Netherlands.

故 宫
The Imperial Palace

故宫旧称紫禁城，是中国明清时代皇帝的宫殿。午门是紫禁城的正门，东、北、西三面城台相连，环抱成一个方形广场。午门正中门楼有左右两座阙亭，内置钟鼓，皇帝祭于坛时鸣钟，祭于庙时击鼓，举行大典时则钟鼓齐鸣。

在午门上看午门，刘谦功摄
Watching Wumen on Wumen, photographed by Liu Qiangong

Previously known as the Forbidden City, *Gugong* (Chinese name for the Imperial Palace) was the imperial palace of generations of emperors from the Ming Dynasty to the Qing Dynasty. The Wumen (Meridian Gate) is the main gate of *Gugong*. It joins the eastern, northern and western wings to form a square. Bells and drums are installed in the two pavilions on the central tower above the Wumen. The bell rang when the emperor was offering sacrifices on the altar, while the drum was played when offering sacrifices in the temple. On occasions of grand ceremonies, the bell and drum would sound simultaneously.

宫殿是古代帝王居住的高大、华丽的房屋，封建社会皇权至高无上，反映到宫殿建筑中，便形成了雄伟壮观、富丽堂皇的风格。从秦始皇的阿房宫到明清紫禁城，尽管历时2000余年，也经历了无数次的改朝换代，但其基本特征是一脉相承的。

Imperial palaces are grand and magnificent houses accommodating ancient emperors and their households. In feudal China, emperors enjoyed supreme authority. This is reflected in the construction of imperial palaces featuring magnificent and splendid styles. Starting from the construction of the Epang Palace in the Qin Dynasty to the Forbidden City in Ming and the Qing dynasties, Chinese history had witnessed countless replacements of dynasties

故宫角楼，田琨摄
A turret in Gugong, photographed by Tian Kun

in a span of over 2000 years; however, the basic features of these two palaces can still be traced to the same origin.

As the imperial palaces of the Ming and Qing dynasties, *Gugong* is also the largest and most complete preservation of ancient architectural complex existing in China. Forming a structurally integrated whole with Beijing City, the palace gradually extends inwards and upwards, imposing on people a sense of stepping into heaven from the earthly world until reaching the place of the "Son of Heaven", which represents the supreme imperial power.

　　故宫是明、清两代的皇宫，也是中国现存最大、最完整的古建筑群，它在结构上与北京城浑然一体，用逐步向内、向上发展的手法，使人如同从人间走向天堂，直至"天子"所在的地方，象征着至高无上的皇权。

　　故宫于明永乐四年（1406）开始建造，永乐十八年（1420）建成，虽经明、清两代多次重修和扩建，但仍保持原来的布局；占地72万平方米，有9000多间房屋，宫墙长约3000米，墙外有52米宽的护城河环绕，是一座壁垒森严的城堡；明清两代——从1420年建成至1911年清朝统治结束——491

Construction of the *Gugong* began in the 4th year of the Yongle period (1406) and was completed in the 18th year (1420). Despite constant reconstruction and expansion, the palace still retains its original layout. The palace covers an area of 720,000 square meters and contains more than 9,000 houses. The palace wall measures about 3,000 meters long, with a 52-meter wide moat circulating around, forming a strongly fortified castle. In the Ming and Qing dynasties, starting from the completion of the palace in 1420 to the end of Qing Dynasty's rule in 1911, twenty-four emperors had lived here where they executed their administrative power.

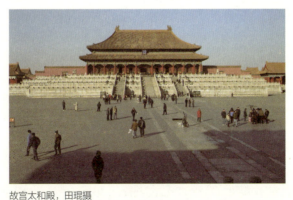

故宫太和殿，田琨摄
The Hall of Supreme Harmony, photographed by Tian Kun

年间先后有24位皇帝在这里居住并执政。

具体说来，故宫宫殿的建筑布局有外朝、内廷之分。外朝以太和、中和、保和三大殿为中心，是皇帝举行大典、召见群臣的地方。内廷有乾清宫、交泰殿、坤宁宫和东西六宫等，是皇帝处理日常政务和后妃、皇子们居住的地方。故宫中轴线末端还有一座御花园，园内的小路很有意思，是用不同颜色的卵石铺成的，组成了900多幅

故宫御花园中的小路，刘谦功摄
A path in the Imperial Garden of Gugong, photographed by Liu Qiangong

图案，内容有人物、花卉、景物、戏剧、典故等，一路看下来妙趣无穷。

与同一时期欧洲建筑相比，中国建筑"淡于宗教与浓于伦理，说明中国文化的哲学超越意识，基本上是现实、现世的，缺乏一种从现实大地向宗教天国之狂热的宗教性的向上

Specifically, the layout of *Gugong* is divided into the Outer Court and Inner Court. The Outer Court centers around the Hall of Supreme Harmony, the Hall of Central Harmony, and the Hall of Preserving Harmony, and was the place where the emperor held grand ceremonies and summoned his ministers. Comprising the Palace of Heavenly Purity, the Hall of Union, the Palace of Earthly Tranquility and the six palaces to the east and west, the Inner Court was the place where the emperor dealt with day-to-day state affairs and was also the residence for concubines and princes. At one end of *Gugong*'s axis is an Imperial Garden lined with interesting paths paved with cobbles of different colors. These cobbles constitute over 900 pictures depicting certain characters, flowers, scenery, dramas and classical allusions. Walking along the path, visitors would experience enormous delight.

Compared with its contemporary western counterparts, Chinese architecture "laid little emphasis on religious elements but stressed the code of ethics. This defines the Chinese philosophy of transcendental consciousness as basically realistic and temporal. It lacks a kind of religious 'pulling force' elevating people from the earthly reality to a religious paradise of passion. Chinese people believe that since the immense happiness of life resides on the realistic earth, there is no need to construct towering architectures in the hope of 'conversing with' the 'harmonious' heaven of religion by means of pointed roofs represented in western medieval churches."[1]

① See *The Cultural Course of Chinese Architecture*, Shanghai People's Press, 2000, pp. 7-8.

'提拉之力'。人们相信，人生之无尽的欢愉既然在现实大地之上，就不必使建筑物高耸入云，以西方中世纪教堂那样的尖顶去与'和美'的宗教天国'对话'。"①因而中国宫殿建筑热衷于在地面上向四处进行有序的铺开，明清故宫紫禁城便是极好的例证。这种建筑空间与平面布局的有序性在于讲究建筑个体与群体组合的风水地理，象征严肃而宁和的人间伦理秩序，乃至帝王至高无上的权威。

Because of this, Chinese palaces are constantly designed as complexes stretching orderly in the four directions of the ground. The Forbidden City of the Ming and Qing dynasties is a perfect exemplification of this point. This kind of order retained between the building space and plane layout finds its value in the geomancy emphasizing the integration of individual buildings and the whole complex. This geomancy symbolizes the solemn and tranquil moral order of the world, and even the supreme authority of feudal emperors.

三言两语 A FEW REMARKS

小时候我跟爸爸妈妈说，我想去乾隆他们家看看，爸爸妈妈就带我去了。后来我才知道，乾隆他们家正式的名字过去叫紫禁城，现在叫故宫。故宫真大，走一天都走不完，就像中国悠久的历史；故宫真气派，须仰视才见的东西太多了，所以常用"庄严雄伟"来形容。

[中国] 龙宝，男，研究生

When I was young, I once told my parents that I want to see Emperor Qianlong's house, so they took me there. Later I learned that the official name of his house was the Forbidden City, which is called *Gugong* (Imperial Palace) now. The *Gugong* is so big that one is impossible to visit the entirety of it in one day, just as the long-standing Chinese history. The *Gugong* is so impressive and contains so many things which have to be viewed by lifting one's eyes, so we often use the word "庄严雄伟" (majestic) to describe the palace.

[China] Long Bao, male, graduate student

不知从什么时候开始，我对故宫情有独钟，只要去北京就要去故宫转一转。可能是受高三时一口气看完的小说《梦回大清》的影响吧，我对四阿哥和十三阿哥住的地方充满了喜爱。我觉得不管你去多少次故宫，变的只能是陪在你身边的人，不变的是紫禁城永远的神秘和庄严。

[中国] 曹春华，女，大学生

I didn't know when I started to develop a special spiritual bond with the *Gugong*. Whenever I go to Beijing, I go and visit the palace. Maybe, this influence came from the book *A Dream Back to Qing Dynasty* that I finished in a single reading. After that I came to love the place where the 4th and 17th princes once lived. In my opinion, no matter how many times you go to *Gugong*, the only thing that changes is the people around you; however, the eternal mystery and majesty of the Forbidden City will remain unchanged.

[China] Cao Chunhua, female, college student

---

①参见王振复，《中国建筑的文化历程》，上海人民出版社，2000年版，第7—8页。

我第一次去故宫感到特别震撼的是它的"大"，包括建筑的大和皇帝权力的大，尽管以前在电影和电视里都看到过故宫，知道它很大，但真的走在故宫里面觉得自己以前的想象不够，看来中国古代的皇帝真的是至高无上的，想干什么就干什么。

[瑞士] 菲利浦，男，大学生

The thing that shocked me upon my first visit to *Gugong* was its "grandness", including the massive size of building and the supreme authority of the emperors. Though I have seen the massiveness of *Gugong* in films and television programs, I felt my original imagination was too conservative. It seems that ancient Chinese emperors had absolute authority thus could do anything they wanted.

[Switzerland] Phillip, male, college student

小链接 ADDITIONAL INFORMATION

凡尔赛宫位于法国巴黎西南部，17世纪由路易十四下令修建。宫殿西面是一座风格独特的法兰西式花园，大小道路都是笔直的，风景十分秀丽。凡尔赛宫外部宏伟壮观，内部装潢考究，200多间房屋金碧辉煌，墙面多由五彩大理石镶制，宫室里吊着各种巨型水晶灯，晶莹璀璨。主要宫殿的墙壁和天花板上遍布壁画和天顶画，题材主要是神话故事和国王战绩。凡尔赛宫及其园林堪称法国古典建筑的杰出代表。

Located in the southwest of Paris in France, the Palace of Versailles was constructed in the 17th century following Louis XIV's decree. West of the palace is a French garden with unique style. Intersected by straight roads and paths, the garden possesses magnificent beauty. The Palace of Versailles has splendid exterior as well as exquisite interior decorations. There are more than 200

法国巴黎的凡尔赛宫
The Palace of Versailles in Paris, France

resplendent chambers whose walls are mostly inlayed with colorful marbles. Various kinds of crystal chandeliers hang on the ceilings inside the palace halls, glittering with brilliance. The walls and ceilings of the main palace are full of murals and paintings depicting myths and the king's military exploits. The Palace of Versailles, together with its garden is an outstanding representative of the French classical architecture.

乐山大佛
The Leshan Giant Buddha

导入 INTRODUCTION

在佛教中，菩萨的地位仅次于佛，是协助佛传播佛法、救助众生的人物。佛教有四大菩萨，即地藏菩萨、普贤菩萨、文殊菩萨、观音菩萨。中国的信徒们为他们建立了各自的道场，即山西五台山的文殊道场、四川峨眉山的普贤道场、浙江普陀山的观音道场、安徽九华山的地藏道场。

峨眉山普贤菩萨金像
The gold statue of Samantabhabra on Mount Emei

In Buddhism, a bodhisattva ranks only lower than the Buddha and is a figure assisting the Buddha in spreading his teachings and relieving all living creatures of earthly sufferings. There are four great Buddhist bodhisattvas, namely Ksitigarbha (bodhisattva of earth treasury), Samantabhadra (bodhisattva of universal worthy), Manjushri (bodhisattva of wisdom) and Avalokiteshvara (the bodhisattva of compassion). Chinese Buddhism followers constructed sacred abodes for all these bodhisattvas, namely Manjushri's abode on Mount Wutai in Shanxi Province, Samantabhadra's abode on Mount Emei in Sichuan Province, Avalokiteshvara's abode on Mount Putuo in Zhejiang Province and Ksitigarbha's abode on Mount Jiuhua in Anhui Province.

峨眉山是普贤菩萨的道场，然而乐山大佛更加气派和壮观。1996年12月6日，峨眉山—乐山大佛作为文化与自然双重遗产被联合国教科文组织列入世界遗产名录。

乐山大佛雕凿在岷江、青衣江和

Mount Emei is the abode of Samantabhadra, however the Leshan Giant Buddha is more impressive and magnificent. On December 6th 1996, the Mount Emei Scenic Area, including Leshan Giant Buddha Scenic Area was indoctrinated into the UNESCO World Heritage List as a cultural and natural heritage item.

壮观的乐山大佛
The magnificent Leshan Giant Buddha

大渡河汇流处的岩壁上，是世界上最大的石刻弥勒佛坐像。佛像开凿于唐玄宗开元初年（713），是海通禅师为减杀水势、普渡众生而集人力、物力、财力修凿的。海通禅师圆寂后工程被迫停止，多年后又由剑南西川节度使章仇兼琼和韦皋续建，至唐德宗贞元19年（803）完工，历时90年。乐山大佛极其壮观，被誉为"山是一尊佛，佛是一座山"。

　　乐山大佛临江危坐，头顶高天，足踏大江，体态匀称，神情肃穆。大佛通高71米，头高14.7米，耳长6.7米，肩宽24米，手指长8.3米，脚背宽9米，仅脚面即可围坐百人以上。大佛左右两侧沿江崖壁上有两尊高达16米的护法天王石刻，与大佛一起形成了一佛二天王的格局。此外还有数百龛上千尊石刻造像，构成了庞大的佛教石刻艺术群。大佛左侧沿"洞天"下去是近代开凿的凌云栈道的始

Carved out of a hillside that lies at the confluence of the Minjiang, Qingyi and Dadu rivers, the Leshan Giant Buddha is the world's largest stone sculpture of a seated Maitreya Buddha. Construction of the Buddha began in the first year of Emperor Xuanzong's rule in the Tang Dynasty (713). The undertaking was led by a Chinese monk named Haitong who collected labors, goods and funding to construct the Buddha with the hope of taming turbulent waters and rescuing all creatures. After his death, however, the construction was unexpectedly suspended. Many years later, Zhangchou Jianqiong and Wei Gao, two *jiedushi* (regional military governors) in Sichuan Province resumed the construction which was eventually completed in the 19th year of Emperor Dezong of the Tang Dynasty (803). Altogether, the construction lasted for 90 years. The Leshan Giant Buddha is extraordinarily spectacular and was extolled by people with the saying "the mountain is a Buddha and the Buddha is a mountain".

Carved with a perfect symmetry, the giant Buddha sits solemnly overlooking the river, with his head reaching the hilltop and feet resting above the rivers. At 71 meters high, the Buddha has a head measuring 14.7 meters tall; his ears are 6.7 meters long, shoulders 24 meters wide, fingers 8.3 meters long; his 9-meter wide insteps are able to accommodate over one hundred people sitting around in concentric circles. On the two cliffs on the left and right sides of the Buddha are carved two 16-meter statues of

端，全长近500米；右侧是唐代开凿大佛时留下的施工和礼佛通道——九曲栈道。佛像雕成后曾建有七层楼阁，唐称"大佛阁"，宋称"凌云阁"，元称"宝鸿阁"……遗憾的是未留存至今，但仍可从大佛两侧的山崖上看到屋檐的痕迹。

乐山大佛的脚趾
The tiptoes of the Leshan Giant Buddha

沿大佛左侧的凌云栈道可直接到达大佛的底部，在此抬头仰望大佛会有仰之弥高的感觉；右侧的九曲栈道沿绝壁开凿而成，蜿蜒而上可登上栈道的顶端，也就是大佛头部的右侧和凌云山的山顶，在此处可观赏到大佛

乐山大佛头部特写
A close-up shot of the Leshan Giant Buddha

Heavenly Kings, forming a pattern called "one Buddha and two Heavenly Kings". In addition, there are hundreds of niches accommodating over a thousand stone statues, constituting an art complex of Buddhist stone-carving. Descending along Dongtian (a cave where the sky can be seen from a fissure on top) on the left side of the Buddha is the beginning part of the 500-meter Lingyun plank road built in modern times. Built in the Tang Dynasty when the construction was started, the Jiuqu plank road on the right side of the Buddha was the passage used for transporting construction materials and worshipping Buddha. Upon completion of the Buddha statue, a seven-story pavilion was once built, which was called the Giant Buddha Pavilion in the Tang Dynasty, Lingyun Pavilion in the Song Dynasty and Baohong Pavilion in the Yuan Dynasty. Unfortunately, the pavilion was not preserved to present day. Nevertheless, we can still discover traces of its eaves from cliffs on the two sides of the Buddha.

Walking downward in the Lingyun plank road, one can directly reach the base of the giant Buddha. Looking up at the Buddha from here, one can be profoundly impressed by its considerable height. Climbing up the meandering Jiuqu plank road built on the right-side cliff, people can ascend to the top of the road, namely the right side of the Buddha head and also the summit of Lingyun Mountain where people can admire the sculpturing skills manifested by the head of the Buddha. Viewed at a distance, the 1,051 chignons on the crown of the Buddha seem to be a monolithic whole, but were actually inlayed one after another.

头部的雕刻艺术。大佛头顶共有螺髻1051个，远看与头部浑然一体，实则是逐一嵌就的。

唐代崇拜弥勒佛①，故将乐山大佛雕成一尊弥勒佛像。佛经说弥勒出世就会"天下太平"，中国唯一的女皇帝武则天曾下令编造《大云经疏》，证明她是弥勒转世，百姓对弥勒的崇拜帮助她在男尊女卑的封建时代登上帝位。由于武则天的大力提倡，全国盛行雕凿弥勒之风。乐山大佛的修造距武则天时代仅20余年，所以当年海通和尚修造乐山大佛时自然选择了弥勒佛，同时弥勒佛是能带来光明和幸福的未来佛，这同老百姓的信仰是一致的。

As the Maitreya Buddha① was revered in the Tang Dynasty, the Leshan Giant Buddha was carved to be a statue depicting the Maitreya Buddha. According to the sutras, the birth of Maitreya will bring "peace and harmony to the world". As a result of this, Wu Zetian, the only empress in China decreed the compilation of *Dayun Sutra* which secured her place as the reincarnation of Maitreya. In a feudal era of patriarchy, the public worship of Maitreya facilitated her taking of the throne. Under Empress Wu Zetian's vigorous promotion, a trend of Maitreya-carving prevailed across the country. The construction of the Leshan Giant Buddha was only some 20 years earlier than Empress Wu Zetian's reign, so the monk Haitong readily adopted the Maitreya Buddha as the prototype for the Leshan Giant Buddha; moreover, Maitreya is a future Buddha bringing people light and happiness, thus the construction was in accordance with the belief of the masses.

三言两语 A FEW REMARKS

大佛宝相庄严，古人用心之虔诚、修造之艰辛令人叹为观止！沿九曲栈道蜿蜒而下，最窄处仅容一人通行，更显山之陡峭、佛之壮观。细观大佛，不得不为古人之胸怀、勇气、技艺所折服。

[中国] 张志向，男，会计

我去乐山听到一个关于大佛的传说，说这里三江会流，总是有船在这里沉下去。为了避免更多的灾难发生，于是修建了大佛，以后居然再也没有船在这个流域出事了。不管真

The solemn giant Buddha constructed out of ancient people's piety and constant effort strikes people with a breathtaking effect. Descending from the winding Jiuqu plank road, the narrowest part allows only one person to pass through, showing the arduousness of the mountain and magnificence of the Buddha. While admiring the Buddha in great detail, I am deeply impressed by ancient people's ambition, courage and skills.

[China] Zhang Zhixiang, male, accountant

I heard a story about the Giant Buddha while visiting Leshan. According to the story, there are always passing boats sinking into the water at the conflux of the three rivers. In order to prevent disasters from happening, the Giant Buddha was erected. From then on, there were no more

---

①弥勒佛：佛教八大菩萨之一，是释迦牟尼佛的继任者，将在未来娑婆世界降生成佛，成为娑婆世界的下一尊佛。

① The Maitreya Buddha, as one of the Eight Bodhisattvas in Buddhism, is the successor of Shakyamuni. Maitreya will be born in the Saha World (the world of endurance) where he will become the next Buddha.

假，我很喜欢这个传说，它让这尊大佛更神秘了。

[中国] 钱晓，女，学生

乐山大佛拥有巨大的身体，我听说大佛从头到脚跟波音747客机一样长，耳朵里可以放进一头长颈鹿，50名士兵可以在它的膝上一字排开，自由女神像也只够得着大佛的肩膀。我在它面前显得很渺小，这是伟大的艺术杰作，人们应该以敬畏之心来观赏。

[美国] 霍尔，男，游客

accidents in the area. No matter whether it is true or not, I love the story because it makes the Buddha even more mysterious.

[China] Qian Xiao, female, student

The Leshan Giant Buddha has a massive body. I once heard that measuring from its head to its feet, the Buddha is as long as a Boeing 747 airliner. Its ears are capable of containing a giraffe, and its knees are able to accommodate 50 soldiers standing in a line. The Statue of Liberty is only as tall as the Giant Buddha's shoulders. Standing below the Buddha, I felt so humble. This is a masterpiece which deserves people's respect and awe.

[USA] Hall, male, tourist

小链接 ADDITIONAL INFORMATION

峨眉山位于中国四川省，最高峰万佛顶海拔3099米，地势陡峭，风景秀丽，有"秀甲天下"之美誉。峨眉山气候多样，植被丰富，共有3000多种植物，包括许多世界上的稀有品种。山路沿途有很多猴群，常结队向游人讨食，成为峨眉山一大特色。峨眉山是中国四大佛教名山之一，作为普贤菩萨的道场，有寺庙26座，佛事频繁，从唐代到今天一直是佛教圣地。

峨眉山的云海
Clouds sea on Mount Emei

Situated in China's Sichuan Province, the Wanfo summit of Mount Emei stands an altitude of 3,099 meters; the steep terrain contains striking scenic beauty and is honored as "the most picturesque place across China". Mount Emei is notable for its diverse climate as well as exceptionally rich vegetation comprising over 3,000 plants including many rare species. The scene of monkeys gathering in crowds along the mountain path to plead for food from the tourists has become a unique feature of Mount Emei. As one of the four major Buddhist mountains in China, Mount Emei is the abode of Samantabhadra. Twenty-six Buddhist temples swarming with worshippers carrying out religious undertakings are scattered on the mountain which has always been a sacred place for Buddhism.

Folk Arts

民间工艺

中国结
Chinese Knot

导入 INTRODUCTION

天宫一号舱内挂件：中国结（截自央视信号）
The pendant in the cabin of Tiangong-1: Chinese knot (from CCTV)

天宫一号是中国第一个目标飞行器和空间实验室，于2011年9月29日成功发射。在天宫一号的舱内醒目地挂着一个大大的中国结。"中国结上凝聚了中国传统文化，它所代表的平安、团圆、祥和的寓意，也恰好代表了研制团队对天宫一号和整个载人航天工程的美好祝愿！"①

Tiangong-1 was successfully launched on September 29th, 2011, as the first target spacecraft and space lab in China. A strikingly big Chinese knot was hung in the cabin of Tiangong-1. "The Chinese knot embodies traditional Chinese culture and its meaning of peace, reunion, and harmony exactly represents the researching team's best wishes for Tiangong-1 and the whole manned space flight project!"①

　　一根红绳，就这么三缠两绕；一种祝福，就这样编结而成。如今的中国结就像中国的书法、绘画、雕刻、陶瓷、菜肴一样，很容易被外国人辨认出来是中国的东西。中国结已成为中华民族的一种符号——像龙凤、长城、黄河一样，体现着中华民族的精神。

Just by twining a red string, the wish is conveyed. Nowadays, the Chinese knot can be easily recognized as something with Chinese characteristics by foreigners just like Chinese calligraphy, painting, sculpture, pottery and food. The

福字形龙凤结，田琨摄
A "福" (fortune) -shaped dragon-phoenix Chinese knot, photographed by Tian Kun

---

①中国航天科技集团公司空间实验室系统副总设计师白明生接受记者采访时所说，见《北京晚报》2011年9月29日文章《天宫一号将搭载一枚中国结飞上太空》。

① Said by Bai Mingsheng, deputy chief engineer of space lab system of China Aerospace Science and Technology Corporation, to the reporter. Seen in "Tiangong-1 Will Carry a Chinese Knot into Space" published in *Beijing Evening News* on September 29th, 2011.

中国结是中国特有的民间手工编织装饰品，起源于上古先民的结绳记事。根据《易·系辞》记载："上古结绳而治，后世圣人易之以书契①。"东汉（25—220）郑玄在《周易注》中说："结绳为约，事大，大结其绳；事小，小结其绳。"作为装饰艺术的中国结则始于唐宋（618—907），盛于明清（1368—1911）。

"结"是一个表示力量、和谐而又充满情感的字眼，无论是结合、结交、结缘还是团结，都给人一种团圆、亲密、温馨的感觉。此外，"结"的发音与"吉"相近，隐含着丰富的文化内涵，如福、禄、寿、喜、财、安、康等等，因此"结"也就自然作为中国文化的表现形式流传至今。

中国结的特点是"一线到底"，即每个中国结从头到尾都是用一根线编织而成的。人们有时把不同的结饰组合在一起，或和其他具有吉祥图案的饰物搭配组合，形成了造型独特、绚丽多彩、寓意深刻的中国传统吉祥装饰物品。

中国结的寓意主要来自两个方面：一是取自结饰形状，二是取自谐音。如："盘长结"寓意长命百岁，"如意结"寓意万事称心，

Chinese knot has become a symbol of the Chinese nation and reflects the national spirit just like the dragon and the phoenix, as well as the Great Wall and the Yellow River.

The Chinese knot is a folk hand-woven ornament peculiar to China and originated from ancient people's keeping records by tying knots. According to "Xi Ci" in *The Book of Changes*, "ancient people ruled the country by means of keeping records by tying knots. Sages of later generations replaced knots with *shuqi*① ". Zheng Xuan of the Eastern Han Dynasty (25-220) wrote in *Notes of the Book of Changes* that "Tying knots implies an agreement. The knot is big if the thing at hand is quite important and the knot is small if the thing at hand is not that important." The Chinese knot was used as an ornamental work of art since the Tang and Song dynasties (618-907) and flourished in the Ming and Qing dynasties (1368-1911).

The Chinese character of "结"（knot）is a word expressing power, harmony, and full of affection. "结合" (unite), "结交" (make friends with), "结缘" (form ties of affection) and "团结" (unity) all give people a feeling of reunion, intimacy and warmth. Moreover, "结" has a similar pronunciation with "吉" (good fortune) and embodies rich cultural connotations such as luck, good job, wealth, longevity, happiness, peace and health. Therefore, the knot naturally remains today as a manifestation of Chinese culture.

The feature of the Chinese knot is that every

---

①书契：指上古时代的文书。

① *Shuqi* refers to documents in ancient times.

中国结"双喜临门"、"吉庆有余"
Chinese knots symbolizing "two happy events coming one after the other" and "jubilancy and abundance"

"双喜结"寓意双喜临门，"团圆结"寓意团圆美满，"双鱼结"寓意吉庆有余，"平安结"寓意一生平安，"吉祥结"寓意吉人天相，等等。

在现代生活中，中国结已发展成为一种多元化的产品和装饰元素，主要包括吉祥挂饰和编结服饰两大系列，吉祥挂饰如居室挂件、汽车挂件等，编结服饰如戒指、耳坠、手链、项链、腰带、盘扣等，它们传承着中国文化、美化了人们今天的生活。

缀有中国结的普洱茶
Pu'erh tea decorated with Chinese knot

Chinese knot is made with only one string. Sometimes people put different knots together or put them together with other ornaments with auspicious patterns, thus forming traditional Chinese auspicious decorations with unique shapes, bright colors, and deep meanings.

The Chinese knot got its meaning mainly due to its shape and homophony. For example, the Panchang Knot means long life. The Ruyi Knot means that everything will go well. The Shuangxi Knot means that two happy events come at the same time. The Tuanyuan Knot means reunion and happiness. The Shuangyu Knot means jubilancy and abundance. The Ping'an Knot means peaceful life. The Jixiang Knot means that heaven rewards the good.

In modern life, the Chinese knot has become a diversified product and decoration, mainly including a lucky pendant such as a pendant in the living room and in the car and a knitting ornament such as ring, eardrop, bracelet, necklace, belt and *pankou* (a kind of button). They inherit Chinese culture and beautify people's life at present.

三言两语 A FEW REMARKS

很多民俗艺术需要心手相传，祖传与拜师格外重要，而中国结则不同，它没有深奥的技巧，只要用心去悟，谁都能做好。中国结至今已经传承了数千年，历史上有不少好作品，只要史书上有记载的，我就琢磨着如何去编制。无论多么精美的中国结，说到底都是简单图案的组合，所以编织中国结，最重要的是用心。

[中国] 尹崇芹，女，中国结艺人

我从小就喜欢手工，手工里面最爱中国结。编结的乐趣在于在这个过程中你必须全神贯注，琢磨每个位置线的走向和顺序。无论怎样复杂的结形，都是一根线从头到尾，虽然纵横交错，却必须井然有序。少一步，错一步，就得重头再来，这美丽的中国结中也蕴涵着人生哲理呢。

[中国] 徐蕾，女，国家公务员

我现在在中国上大学，每次放假回家的时候都要给朋友们带礼物，中国结往往是我的第一选择，因为我觉得在好带的礼品里，中国结的颜色和含义都最能代表中国。我在俄罗斯的朋友们都很喜欢中国结，他们中间来过中国的不多，但通过中国结开始对中国有一些了解了。

[俄罗斯] 安娜，女，大学生

Many folk arts need to be passed on by means of teach-by-doing. Therefore, handing the art down from the ancestors and taking somebody as the teacher are especially important. Chinese knots, however, are different because they require no complicated skills yet attention and effort. The Chinese knot has a history of thousands of years and many good Chinese knots were made in the past. I always ponder how to make different Chinese knots recorded in historical books. All Chinese knots, no matter how exquisite, are combinations of simple patterns. Therefore, the most important thing in making Chinese knots is to pay attention and make effort.

[China] Yin Chongqin, female, Chinese knot maker

I have loved handworks since my childhood and like Chinese knots most. The interesting thing about making Chinese knots is that you have to concentrate your whole attention on it during the process and think about how and where to put the string all the time. Every Chinese knot is made with only one string no matter how complicated it is. Although it is arranged in a crisscross pattern, it must follow a certain order. You have to start again if you omit a step or make a mistake. The beautiful Chinese knot does embody life philosophy.

[China] Xu Lei, female, civil servant

I attend the university in China now and bring gifts for my friends every time I return home. The Chinese knot is always my primary choice because it is easy to take and its color and meaning can represent China most. All of my friends in Russia love Chinese knots very much and know something about China through Chinese knots though many of them have never been in China.

[Russia] Anna, female, university student

小链接 ADDITIONAL INFORMATION

　　盘扣是中国结的一种，元明（1206—1644）以后，人们渐渐用盘扣来连接衣襟，题材多取自具有民族情趣和吉祥意义的图案。盘扣花式很丰富，有模仿植物的菊花扣、梅花扣，盘结成文字的"吉"字扣、"寿"字扣、"囍"字扣，采用几何图形的一字扣、波形扣、三角形扣等。盘扣使用时分列两边，有对称的，也有不对称的。在中国服饰的演化中，盘扣不仅有连接衣襟的功能，更被视为装饰服装的点睛之笔，生动地表现出中国服饰重意蕴、重内涵、重主题的装饰趣味。

旗袍盘扣
The pankou for cheongsam

As a kind of Chinese knot, *pankou* was used to fasten the front of a garment since the Yuan and Ming dynasties (1206-1644). Its subjects are mostly derived from the images with national interest holding auspicious meanings. *Pankou* has a variety of shapes including plant-shaped ones such as the chrysanthemum-shaped *pankou* and plum blossom-shaped *pankou*, Chinese character-shaped ones such as "吉" (good fortune)-shaped *pankou*, "寿" (long life)-shaped *pankou* and "囍" (double happiness)-shaped *pankou*, and those of geometric shapes such as linear-shaped *pankou*, wave-shaped *pankou*, and triangle-shaped *pankou*. The *pankou* is used on the two sides of the clothes either symmetrically or asymmetrically. In the evolution of Chinese clothes, the *pankou* is not only used to fasten the front of a garment but also regarded as the focal point in the decorating of clothes. It vividly reflects Chinese people's decoration tastes which emphasize implications, connotations and subjects.

皮 影
Shadow Play

导入 INTRODUCTION

皮影戏是一种极具中国特色的民间艺术，2010年5月，在上海世博会开幕式上，唐山皮影剧团进行了8场巡演，把《鹤与龟》、《沉香救母》、《观世音传奇》三大经典历史传说剧目及《大闹天宫》的选场奉献给了中外宾客，后者还采用了全英文台词，赢得了中外观众一阵阵掌声和喝彩声。

世博园区内宝钢大舞台上演的《鹤与龟》
Crane and Tortoise played in BaoSteel Stage in the Expo Park

Shadow play is a folk art with distinctive Chinese features. In the opening ceremony of the Expo 2010 Shanghai China in May 2010, the Tangshan Shadow Play Theater went up for eight rounds and presented to the Chinese and foreign audience three classic historical legend plays—*Crane and Tortoise*, *Chen Xiang Saves His Mother* and *Legends of God of Mercy* as well as some all-English selected scenes of the *Havoc in Heaven*, winning bursts of applause and cheers.

皮影戏是中国民间传统艺术，在没有电影与电视的时代，皮影戏是十分受欢迎的民间娱乐活动。

所谓皮影戏，是一种用灯光照射兽皮或纸板做成的人物剪影表演故事的民间戏曲形式。表演时艺人们在白色幕布后面一边操纵戏曲人物，一边用当地流行的曲调唱述故事，同时配以打击乐

As a form of Chinese folk art, shadow play was a very popular folk entertaining activity when there was neither movie nor TV.

Shadow play is a form of folk drama with full-bodied local flavor. It acts out stories by using puppet shadows on lighted hide or paperboard. In performance, actors manipulate the puppets behind the white screen while telling stories in locally popular tune along with percussion and string music.

皮影，李佳琳摄
Shadow puppet, photographed by Li Jialin

器和弦乐，具有浓郁的乡土气息。

皮影发源于西汉时期（前206—公元25）的陕西，作为戏剧演出始于北宋（960—1127），清代（1616—1911）发展到鼎盛时期，皮影戏班遍布全国各地。

皮影一般由驴皮制作。首先要将皮子浸泡、刮薄、磨平，然后将各种人物的图谱描绘在上面，用刀具刻凿成形，再涂上颜色。人物造型与真人表演的戏剧一样，生、旦、净、末、丑角色齐全。皮影人的头和四肢是用线连缀在一起的，以便能够自由活动。皮影艺人不仅手很灵活，嘴上也要会说、会念、会唱，脚下还得制动锣鼓，技艺十分高超。

演皮影的屏幕是一块白布，演出时打上强光，透过灯光的皮影变得通体透明、色泽鲜艳。艺人们通过竹

Shadow play originated from Shaanxi in the Western Han Dynasty (206 BC-AD 25). It was performed as a kind of drama since the Northern Song Dynasty (960-1127) and reached its heyday in the Qing Dynasty (1616-1911) when shadow play troupes were seen all around China.

Most shadow puppets are made of donkey skin. First donkey skin is soaked, scraped and smoothed and then patterns of various human figures are painted on the skin. Later, the puppet takes shape after being carved with knives and colored. The puppets have five types of roles—*sheng, dan, jing, mo* and *chou,* the same as those in real human operas. The head and limbs of the puppet are connected by threads so that it can move freely. Shadow play artists show superb skills because they not only have dexterous hands but also need to play the drum with their feet while speaking, reciting or singing.

皮影的制作
The production of shadow puppet

扦来调动影人，观众则在白幕的另一面看到了活灵活现的形象。皮影戏的内容相当丰富，传统剧目以神话、传说与历史故事为主，如《白蛇传》、《西厢记》、《岳飞传》等等。

The screen for shadow plays is made of a piece of white cloth on which the strong light makes the puppets transparent and brightly-colored in the performance. Artists move the puppets with bamboo spikes so that the audience can see the vivid images on the other side of the white screen. Shadow play is rich in content. Traditional plays are mostly myths, legends and historical stories such as the *Legend of the White Snake*, *Romance of the Western Chamber* and the *Legend of Yue Fei*.

皮影戏后台
The backstage of shadow play

As shadow play has become widely spread across China, its performing and singing style is more or less influenced by arts of different places, thus giving rise to various schools of shadow plays. In Northwest China, with Shaanxi Province where shadow plays originated as its representative, shadow plays there feature slim and pretty character modeling and beautiful and fair-sounding singing. However, in North China and Northeast China as is represented by Hebei Province, traditional shadow play is

　　由于皮影戏在中国流传的地域十分广阔，表演与唱腔风格或多或少受到了各地艺术的影响，形成了形式多样的流派。陕西是中国皮影戏的源头，以其为代表的中国西北部地区皮影精细秀丽，唱腔动听悦耳。以河北为代表的中国华北、东北部地区的传统皮影，造型给人一种淳朴粗犷而又不失典雅的美感，唱腔则浑厚圆润一些。

陕西皮影戏，李佳琳摄
The shadow play in Shaanxi, photographed by Li Jialin

皮影戏是中国最早走出国门、闯入世界的戏剧艺术。自13世纪，中国皮影戏便随军事远征和海陆交往相继传入了亚洲的波斯（今伊朗）、阿拉伯、土耳其以及欧洲的英、法、德、意、俄等国，德国文学家歌德与英国表演艺术家卓别林都曾给予中国皮影戏艺术高度的评价。

characterized by simple, unsophisticated but elegant and beautiful character modeling as well as rich and rounded tone.

Shadow play is the first Chinese drama art to go abroad. Since the 13th century, the Chinese shadow play has been successively spread into Persia (now Iran), Arab and Turkey in Asia and England, France, Germany, Italy, and Russia in Europe as a result of military expedition and communication across lands and seas. German writer Goethe and British performing artist Chaplin both spoke highly of Chinese shadow plays.

三言两语 A FEW REMARKS

我喜欢皮影的造型，有一种特别的韵味，那些人物能骑马，能打仗，能生气，能跺脚，其实就是一个小傀儡，可什么都能做，什么都能变。皮影表演起来特别神秘，一盏灯火，一层影窗，皮影一贴幕就来，一脱幕就走，真真假假、虚虚实实，让人产生不尽的联想。

[中国] 路联达，男，民间艺人

I love the modeling of shadow puppets because they have a special styling. Although they are only small puppets, they are able to do anything and be changed into anything. They can ride a horse, fight a battle, become angry and stamp their feet. Shadow play is quite mysterious only with a light and a screen. The shadow puppets are in sight when they get close to the screen and out of sight when they leave the screen. The mixture of truth and falsehood inspires people's endless imagination.

[China] Lu Lianda, male, folk artist

皮影戏真的很神奇，我第一次接触到它时，远远听起来完全是一个几十人组成的大乐队和大剧团，可进到场内一看，只有五个人。他们每个人都操作四五件乐器，看得我眼花缭乱的，他们却忙而不乱。还有那些皮影，活灵活现，甚至连眼睛都会眨。虽然他们唱的我听不懂，但我仍然觉得很有意思。

[德国] 托马斯，男，游客

Shadow play is really amazing. When I was first exposed to it, I felt that it sounded like a band or a troupe made of dozens of people. However, I saw only five people inside the theater. All of them were busy with playing four or five musical instruments but not at random. The scene really dazzled my eyes. The shadow puppets were lifelike and even able to blink their eyes. Although I failed to understand what they were singing, I still found it quite interesting.

[Germany] Thomas, male, visitor

小链接
ADDITIONAL INFORMATION

　　拉洋片是中国的一种民间艺术，又称"西洋镜"。表演时艺人将各种画片装入特制的大木箱中，箱子外壁有若干个圆洞，洞上装一个凸镜，观看者通过凸镜往箱内观看。表演者一边拉放画片，一边根据画面内容配以唱词和锣鼓。在电影尚未普及的年代，拉洋片是一种可以代替电影的娱乐方式，十分受老百姓欢迎。

拉洋片，田琨摄
Peepshow, photographed by Tian Kun

Peepshow, also known as raree show, is a form of Chinese folk art. While performing, the artist puts printed pictures into a big specially-made wooden box which has several holes on its surface. Convex lens are installed in the holes so that people can peep into the box through the holes. The performers show the pictures while singing and playing the drum according to the pictures. During the time when movies had not yet been popularized, peepshow was a highly popular entertaining activity that had the same function as movies.

刺 绣
Chinese Embroidery

在2011年戛纳国际电影节上，中国演员范冰冰身着一件大红色的仙鹤裙装，将中国刺绣的风采完美地展现在世人面前。据说这件衣服动用了70个工人历时4个月才完成。裙装上9只形态各异的仙鹤翩翩起舞，每条纹路都是按照仙鹤羽毛的方向刺绣的，中间缀以梅、兰、竹、菊，更是营造了一种独具中国风格的意境。

仙鹤裙
Red-crowned crane gown

During the Cannes International Film Festival in 2011, the Chinese actress Fan Bingbing wore a bright red "red-crowned crane gown" and perfectly unfolded Chinese embroidery before the eyes of people from all over the world. It is said that 70 people spent four months to make this gown. The nine red-crowned cranes in different shapes on the gown dance trippingly and each line on the gown is embroidered along the feather of the red-crowned cranes. The gown is also embellished with plum blossoms, orchid, bamboo and chrysanthemum in the middle, which creates an artistic mood with unique Chinese features.

刺绣俗称"绣花"，在中国至少有三千年的历史，目前传世最早的刺绣为湖南长沙战国楚墓中出土的绣品。明清（1368—1911）以来具有地域特色的刺绣品种日趋成熟，其中以江苏苏州的苏绣、湖南长沙的湘绣、四川成都的蜀绣、广

Embroidery, also known as *xiuhua* in Chinese, has a history of at least three thousand years. The earliest embroidery that remains today is unearthed from the Chu tomb of the Warring States Period in Changsha, Hunan Province. In the Ming and Qing dynasties (1368-1911), different types of embroideries with local features become increasingly mature,

东潮州的粤绣成就最高、影响最大，被称为"四大名绣"。四大名绣在题材、构图、用线、用色、针法等方面各不相同，但都以追求"画绣"——即绘画效果高度逼真——为最高境界。

苏绣以针脚细密、色彩淡雅而著称，题材以动物为主。双面绣是苏绣的一大特色，如常见的双面绣《小猫》，无论从正面还是反面都可以看到小猫调皮活泼的神态。此外还有多种多样的绣品，如《凤之舞》充分表现出中国人丰富的想象力，更具文化内涵。

湘绣的艺术特色是形象逼真、质感强烈，以针代笔，以线晕色，在画稿的基础上进行再创造，凭借针法的特殊表现力和绣线的光泽使绣制出来的物象不但保存着笔墨神韵，而且增添了物象的真实性和立体感，有"绣花能生香，绣鸟能闻声，绣虎能奔跑，绣人能传神"之说。

苏绣《凤之舞》，田琨摄
Dance of the Phoenix, a Suzhou embroidery, photographed by Tian Kun

among which the four major regional styles of Chinese embroidery—Suzhou embroidery (Su Xiu), Hunan embroidery (Xiang Xiu), Sichuan embroidery (Shu Xiu) and Guangdong embroidery (Yue Xiu) have the greatest achievements and influence. Despite their differences in subject, composition, use of threads and colors, as well as knitting, the four embroideries all regard the quality of being true to life as the highest pursuit.

Suzhou embroidery, whose main subject is animals, is known for its fine close stitch and elegant color. Double-faced embroidery has been a key feature of Suzhou embroidery. For instance, in the common embroidery *Kitten*, one can see the vivid and naughty kitten on both sides of the embroidery. There are also many other kinds of embroideries such as *Dance of the Phoenix* which reflects Chinese people's rich imagination and also embodies rich cultural connotations.

The artistic features of Hunan embroidery are lifelike images and have strong textures. Needles take the place of pens and threads are used to stitch color on the embroidery. Recreated on the basis of the sketch, the image of the embroidery not only has the romantic charm of pens and inks but

湘绣《饮水虎》
The Tiger Drinking Water, a
Hunan embroidery

　　粤绣由黎族初创，至明朝中后期全面成熟，其特色为：用线多样、用色明快、构图丰满，特别讲求华丽的视觉效果。绣品品种非常丰富，有被面、枕套、床楣、披巾、头巾、绣服、鞋帽、戏装等，传统题材多为孔雀和荔枝。

　　蜀绣早在晋代就被称为"蜀中之宝"，针法严谨、片线光亮、针脚平齐、色彩明快，传统针法绣技近100种，人物、花鸟、山水皆能表现，富有立体感和装饰性。

　　刺绣常被用作穿戴的装饰，如鞋面、鞋垫、肚兜、荷包、香包等。刺绣纹样大都隐含着对自然的体现和对生活的热爱。例如，女装袖口多有祥云，裙摆多有花花草

also seems to be lifelike and stereoscopic because of the particularly expressive stitch and the glossy embroidery threads. It is said that "the embroidered flower gives off fragrance; the embroidered bird makes sounds; the embroidered tiger is capable of running; the embroidered human figure is true in spirit."

Guangdong embroidery was created by the Li nationality and fully mature in the middle and late Ming Dynasty. It features multiple usages of threads, bright colors, full composition, and special focus on luxuriant visual effect. The great variety of Guangdong embroideries, whose traditional subjects are mostly peacocks and leeches, include quilt covers, pillowcases, bed lintels, shawls, kerchiefs, clothing, shoes, hats, and stage costumes.

粤绣《松鹤延年》
Longevity Crane, a Guangdong embroidery

Sichuan embroidery was praised as the "Treasure of Shu (another name for Sichuan Province)" as early as the Jin Dynasty. Featuring careful knitting, glossy threads, neat stitch, and bright colors, it has nearly 100 kinds of traditional knitting methods

蜀绣《熊猫》，田琨摄
Panda, a Sichuan embroidery, photographed by Tian Kun

and can show human figures, flowers, birds, landscapes in a stereoscopic and decorative way.

Embroidery is often used as decoration for dresses and accessories such as vamp, shoe-pad, bellyband, small bag and sachet. The decorative patterns of embroideries mostly reflect the nature and the love for life. For example, the sleeve cuff of women's dresses is always decorated with the image of auspicious clouds and their skirt hemlines are often decorated with images of flowers and grass. Bellybands of children in the rural areas are embroidered with red trimmings and images of "lotus and child" and "precious long spring" which represent good fortune and the continuity of life. Boys' bibs are decorated with images of "two tigers with their heads together", "two lions with their heads together" and "five bats (meaning good fortune in Chinese) around the Chinese character '寿' (longevity)"; while girls' bibs are embroidered with images of "five butterflies flying around a flower", "children sitting on the lotus" and "five fish swimming around the lotus".

草。又如，农村儿童的肚兜多是红色镶边的绣花，一般饰有"莲生贵子"、"宝贵长春"等寓意吉祥、子孙繁衍的图案。男孩的围嘴常绣有"双虎对头"、"双狮对头"、"五福捧寿"的图案；女孩的围嘴，则绣以"五蝶捧花"、"五莲坐子"、"五鱼戏莲"等图案。

　　如今，电脑绣花机的出现使传统的手工绣花得到高速度、高效率的实现，并且还能实现手工绣花无法达到的"多层次、多功能、统一性和完美性"的要求。

The emergence of the computer embroidery machine contributed to the high speed and the great efficiency of today's embroidery compared with that of traditional hand-made embroidery and it meets the requirements of "multi-level, multi-function, unity and perfection" which surpass hand-made embroidery's reach.

三言两语 A FEW REMARKS

一次去阿勒泰，我看到游客非常喜欢哈萨克族绣品，回来和老婆商量，就搞起了家庭刺绣。先是绣花帽，因为比较简便，后来我就自己设计图案绣挂毯、马甲、书包、靠垫和桌布。现在，我最大的愿望是把女儿培养成接班人，送她去学电脑、学设计，将来在电脑上设计图案会又快又好。还要再招几个帮手，教他们把哈萨克族传统刺绣艺术传承下去。

[中国] 胡尔曼汗，男，
手工艺品店店主

Once I went to Altay and found that visitors loved Kazakh embroidery very much. After returning home, I discussed with my wife and began our family embroidery. We embroidered flowered hats first because they are comparatively easy. Then I designed patterns on my own to embroider tapestry, waistcoat, schoolbag, back cushion, and tablecloths. Now my greatest wish is to train my daughter as my successor and send her to learn computer skills and design so that she will design patterns with high speed and good quality on her computer. I will also hire some assistants who will pass on the traditional Kazakh embroidery taught by me.
[China] Herman Khan, male, owner of a handcraft shop

我的祖母很会刺绣，我小的时候她经常在我的衣服上绣花——说是绣花，其实什么都有，比如开放的花朵、细长的树叶、可爱的小猫、漂亮的小鸟等等。来到中国以后我看到过许多中国的绣品，它们常常让我想起我的祖母，所以回国时我常常会买各种绣品送给我的祖母，她可喜欢了。

[墨西哥] 叶塞尼亚，女，大学生

My grandma is quite good at embroidery. When I was young, she often embroidered flowers on my clothes. In fact, she embroidered not only blooming flowers, but also slender leaves, cute cats, beautiful birds and so on. After arriving in China, I see a lot of Chinese embroidery which reminds me of my grandma. Therefore, when I return to my country, I always buy embroidery for my grandma and she loves it very much.

[Mexico] Yesenia, female, university student

十字绣钱包
Cross-stitched wallets

目前风靡世界的十字绣最早发源于中国唐宋时期的民间工艺"挑花"，14世纪经土耳其传到欧洲，时值文艺复兴时期，挑花因针法简单、表现力强而风靡欧洲各国宫廷。由于挑花以十字交叉针法为主，故被译为"cross-stitch"，即十字绣。15世纪十字绣开始进入民间，逐渐为大众所接受，后来又从欧洲传入美洲、非洲、大洋洲并重返亚洲，20世纪挑花工艺重归故里，被中国人俗称为"十字绣"。

The cross-stitch, which sweeps the world today, originated from the Chinese folk art cross-stitch (*tiaohua*) in the Tang and Song dynasties. It was introduced to Europe via Turkey in the 14th century and prevailed in European palaces because of its simple stitch yet strong expression. It is called the cross-stitch because it is done with pairs of stitches that cross each other. In the 15th century, cross-stitch was spread into the folk and recognized by ordinary people. Later, it was spread from Europe to America, Africa and Oceania and returned to Asia again. In the 20th century, the cross-stitch returned to its native land and was named as *shizixiu* by Chinese people.

面　塑
Dough Modeling

导入 INTRODUCTION

汤夙国的面塑作品：《雕塑大师罗丹》

Master Sculptor Rodin, dough modeling work of Tang Suguo

汤子博是中国著名的面塑大师，他善绘画，精面塑，是"面人汤"的创始人，不仅面人，他还涉猎金、石、泥、木等多种造型艺术。其子汤夙国——"面人汤"第二代传人——亦苦心钻研雕塑艺术，并遍行欧美，在传播中华民族传统艺术的同时还潜心研究各国艺术，作品《雕塑大师罗丹》体现了其融汇中西的艺术风格，1996年联合国教科文组织授予汤夙国先生"民间工艺美术大师"称号。

Tang Zibo, a famous Chinese master of dough modeling, is proficient in painting and dough modeling. As the creator of Tang's Dough Figurine, he is involved not only in dough modeling but also in gold, stone, mud and wood modeling. His son Tang Suguo, the second generation of Tang's Dough Figurine, also takes pains to study sculpture and travels around the world. While spreading traditional Chinese folk art, he also studies the art of different countries and forms a style that fuses Chinese and Western art, which is reflected in his work *Master Sculptor Rodin*. In 1996, UNESCO awarded him the title of Master of Chinese Folk Arts & Crafts.

面塑俗称"捏面人"，它以调成不同颜色的糯米面为主料，用手和简单的工具塑造出各种栩栩如生的形象。

Dough modeling is commonly known as *nie mianren* (making dough figurines). With sticky rice flour of different colors as the main ingredient, it creates various vivid images only with hands and simple tools.

面塑始于汉代（前206—公元220），盛于清代（1616—1911），是深受民间喜爱的玩偶。面塑源于民间在喜庆日子里做的一些喜馍馍、花点心，久而久之便形成了独特的民间艺术，历经几千年而不衰。20世纪初在北京有专制大型面塑礼品的铺面，有庆婚的"举案齐眉"，贺子的"榴开百子"，祝寿的"八仙①庆寿"。

面人引来游客驻足欣赏
Visitors stopping to appreciate the dough figurines

面塑形象多为传统戏曲、古典小说、民间传说、神话故事、动画漫画中的人物以及十二生肖和其他动物，如关羽、孙悟空、王母娘娘、葫芦娃、奥特曼等。当然时尚因素也会影响面塑的创作，如2008年北京奥运会的吉祥物"福娃"就被面塑艺人们捏制出来，而且非常受欢迎。

面塑艺术也有不同的风格与流派，如天津的"面人赵"和北京的"面人汤"。"面人赵"的作品细致艳丽，"面人汤"的作品古朴生动。

Dough modeling originated in the Han Dynasty (206 BC-AD 220) and flourished in the Qing Dynasty (1616-1911), enjoying great popularity among people. It stemmed from the steamed bun and dessert that people made in festivals and gradually became a kind of special folk art which has lasted for several thousand years. In the early 20th century, shops in Beijing specially made large-sized dough figurines as gifts, including "husband and wife treating each other with courtesy" to celebrate marriages, "pomegranate bringing many children" to congratulate people regarding having babies and "*baxian*① (Eight Immortals) celebrating the birthday of elderly people" to offer birthday congratulations.

The subjects of dough figurines are mostly the twelve zodiac animals and other animals as well as human figures in traditional operas, folk legends, fairy tales, cartoons and animations such as Guan Yu, Sun Wukong (Monkey King), the Queen Mother, Calabash Brothers and Ultraman. Fashion, of course, will also affect dough modeling. For example, Fuwa, the mascot of the 2008 Beijing Olympic Games, were modeled with dough and gained great popularity.

Dough modeling is also divided into many styles and schools such as the delicate and gorgeous Zhao's Dough Figurine in Tianjin and the simple and vivid Tang's Dough Figurine in Beijing.

Dough figurines can be used not only for

①八仙：源于唐代的民间传说，明朝时流行八仙图，大多为铁拐李、汉钟离、张果老、吕洞宾、何仙姑、蓝采和、韩湘子和曹国舅八位人物。

① *Baxian* (Eight Immortals): originated from the folk legend in the Tang Dynasty when the *Picture of the Eight Immortals* was quite popular. In most cases, they refer to Iron-Crutch Li, Han Zhongli, Elder Zhang Guo, Lü Dongbin, Immortal Woman He, Lan Caihe, Philosopher Ham Xiang, and Royal Uncle Cao.

天津"面人赵"作品《钟馗娶妻》
Zhong Kui (a figure of Chinese mythology) Gets Married, a Zhao's Dough Figurine in Tianjin

除了用于收藏的面塑，还有可以食用的面塑。中国北方以面食为主，因此逢年过节或大小喜庆的日子，人们便纷纷制作出各种形象的面塑，或用于祭祀，或作为礼品赠送给亲友。比如，过春节的时候要做莲花和鱼形的面塑，表示"连年有余"；又如，婚礼上要送龙凤、鸳鸯、石榴形状的"喜饽饽"，祝愿新人生活美满、多子多福。

过去面塑艺人多以街头为工作坊，挑担提盒，走乡串镇，作品虽深受群众喜爱，却被视为一种小玩意儿，不能登大雅之堂。如今面塑艺术已成为珍贵的非物质文化遗产，小玩意儿也走入了艺术殿堂。

collection but also for eating. People in North China mainly eat cooked wheaten food and, during festivals or on other auspicious occasions, make dough figurines of different images as sacrifices to gods and ancestors or gifts to relatives and friends. For instance, the lotus-shaped and fish-shaped dough figurines made during the Spring Festival mean prosperity year after year; steamed buns in the shape of dragon, phoenix, mandrin duck or pomegranate are used as gifts to celebrate marriages and express the wish of a happy life, fertility and good fortune for the new couple.

In the past, dough-modeling artists always worked in streets carrying their load and box through streets and lanes. Despite their great popularity, dough figurines were only regarded as unrefined gadgets. Nowadays, however, dough modeling has been transformed into a kind of precious intangible cultural heritage and the gadget has become artistic and presentable.

鱼形面塑
Fish-shaped dough figurine

面塑艺术有几个特点，首先是体积小，作为旅游纪念品容易携带；第二是精细，面本身细滑而有弹性，可以用来刻画非常细腻的人物表情以及服饰细节；第三是传神，面塑也追求艺术表现力，要对题材稍作变形以传神。工艺嘛，就要有"工"也有"艺"，有技术也有艺术。

[中国] 冯海瑞，男，面塑艺人

我一直卖工艺品，所以对工艺美术情有独钟。去中国旅游时我带回了几个面人，一直爱不释手。我喜欢面人是因为它们太传神了，那么一些微缩的小人儿和戏曲里面的人物比起来一点儿也不逊色，活灵活现地就像真人一样。小动物就更不用说了，小鹿好像随时都可以跑起来，小鸟好像随时都可以飞起来，把它们摆在书桌上觉得自己很贴近大自然。

[新加坡] 陈素芬，女，商场售货员

Dough modeling has several characteristics. First, it is small-sized and portable as a tourist souvenir. Second, the dough is so smooth and elastic that people can depict the nuance of facial expressions and details of clothes on it. Third, being vivid and expressive, dough figurines also pursue artistic expressiveness through making small changes to the subjects. As a kind of craft, it embodies both technological and artistic features.

[China] Feng Hairui, male, dough modeling artist

I've always been selling handicrafts and have special preference to arts and handicrafts. In my travel to China, I bought a few dough figurines and loved them very much because they are very expressive and vivid. The small-sized human figure is quite lifelike and no less vivid than people in operas. Not to mention the small animals such as deer that seem to be about to run at any time and birds that seem to be about to fly at any time. Putting them on the desk, I feel myself close to nature.

[Singapore] Chen Sufen, female, shop assistant

吹糖人是旧时北京的一个行业，小贩们肩挑挑子走街串巷，挑子里有一个小炭炉，炉上大勺中盛满了糖稀，以备吹糖人之用。糖人好看、好玩儿，玩儿完以后还能吃，孩子特别喜欢，见着就走不动了。糖人说是人，其实还有各种动物，如张飞、嫦娥、山羊、金鱼等等，最受孩子喜爱的是孙猴儿（孙悟空）。孙猴儿做好后要在猴背上敲一个小洞，倒入些糖稀，再在其后身扎一个小孔，让糖浆慢慢流出来，下面用一个小江米碗接着，用小江米勺舀碗里的糖稀吃，等糖稀流完后，则可连孙猴儿和江米碗勺一块吃掉。对于孩子来说，这套玩艺可以先看，再玩儿，最后还可以解馋，自然不能放过它了。

吹糖人，田琨摄

Creating a sugar figurine (the step of blowing air into it), photographed by Tian Kun

Sugar figurine used to be a kind of business in Beijing. Peddlers walk through streets and lanes carrying their loads. A charcoal stove is in their loads and the big spoon on the stove is filled with sugar used for making sugar-coated figurines. Children love the figurines very much and stop to buy them because the beautiful and interesting figurines can be admired first and then eaten. The figurines have images of humans such as Zhang Fei and Chang'e as well as various kinds of animals such as goat and goldfish. Children's favorite image is Sun Wukong (Monkey King). To model the image of Sun Wukong, craftsmen will dig a hole on the back of the monkey and pour sugar into the hole. Then they will dig another hole at the bottom of the monkey so that the sugar will flow out of the hole into the bowl under the figurine. The bowl is filled with polished glutinous rice which can be eaten with a spoon. After all sugar flows into the bowl, people can eat both the monkey-shaped sugar figurine and the polished glutinous rice. For children, they will certainly not let the sugar figurine go because they can watch the whole making process, play with the figurine and then eat it.

年 画
New Year Picture

2006年世界杯艺术海报评选是当年全球艺术家们最为关注的事件之一，世界各国近100位顶尖艺术家参与了评选活动，不过最终让德国东道主倾倒的，却是一幅出自罗氏兄弟①之手的中国传统年画——"大力神杯"：一个留着"茶壶盖儿"头发的胖小孩，手中托着一个圆圆的足球，足球的上面贴着几个大大的"福"字，主画面象征着世界杯的奖杯——大力神杯。

中国年画——"大力神杯"
Chinese New Year picture—The Hercules Cup

The 2006 World Cup Poster Competition is among the events that received the most attention from artists all over the world in that year. Nearly 100 top artists in the world took part in the competition. In the end, however, what attracted Germany, the host country, most was a traditional Chinese New Year picture—*The Hercules Cup* drawn by the Luo Brothers①. In the picture, a chubby child with lid-shaped hairstyle held in his hand with a round football with several Chinese characters "福" (good fortune) on it. The main part of the picture represents the trophy of the World Cup—the Hercules Cup.

年画是中国民间绘画独具特色的一个种类，也是中国人喜闻乐见的一种艺术形式。每值岁末，人们盛行在室内贴年画，门上贴门神，用以除旧岁、迎新春，营造欢乐的节日气氛。年画因一年更换一次，或张贴后可供一年欣赏，故而得名。

The New Year picture is a unique kind of Chinese folk painting and an artistic form of great popularity. At the end of each year, people will post New Year pictures up in their homes and door-gods on the doors to ring out the old year, ring in the new year and create a happy and festive atmosphere. The New Year picture

①罗氏兄弟是由来自广西南宁的罗卫东、罗卫国、罗卫兵三兄弟组成的。他们是中国最早与西方接触并受到西方艺术界广泛赞誉的中国当代艺术家，在中国当代艺术界独树一帜，是所谓的艳俗艺术或浮华艺术的代表。

① The Luo Brothers refer to Luo Weidong, Luo Weiguo and Luo Weibing, the three brothers from Nanning, Guangxi Province. As the contemporary Chinese artists first exposed to the West and receiving widespread praise from the Western art world, they developed a school of their own in contemporary Chinese art circles and represent the so-called gaudy art.

苏州桃花坞、天津杨柳青、山东潍坊和四川绵竹是中国著名的年画产地，被誉为"年画四大家"。

苏州桃花坞年画以门神著称，兼有其他种类年画，用一版一色的木版套印方法印刷，主要表现民俗生活、戏文故事、花鸟蔬果、驱鬼避邪等传统内容，在艺术风格上构图丰富，色调艳丽，富有浓郁的生活气息。

桃花坞年画———团和气
New Year picture of Taohuawu—A Prevailing Mood of Harmony

天津杨柳青年画采用木版套印和手工彩绘相结合的方法，色彩斑斓，具有一种特别的人情味和生活气息。杨柳青年画取材广泛，如历史故事、神话传奇、戏曲人物、世俗风情以及山水花鸟等，其中戏曲人物、美女、胖娃娃等形象最为精美传神。

山东潍坊杨家埠年画完全以手工操

绘制中的杨柳青年画
Painting a New Year picture of Yangliuqing type

is called so because it is changed once each year and admired for a whole year after being pasted.

Taohuawu in Suzhou, Yangliuqing in Tianjin, Weifang in Shandong Province, and Mianzhu in Sichuan Province are most famous production places for New Year pictures in China and New Year pictures produced by these four places are called "the four great New Year picture types".

The New Year picture of Taohuawu in Suzhou is famous for its door-god picture and also includes other types of pictures. Printed on a single-colored board through woodblock printing, it mainly reveals traditional contents such as folk life, opera stories, flowers, birds, vegetables, fruits, and images able to drive away evil spirits. It also features rich composition and gorgeous colors in terms of artistic style and contains a rich flavor of life.

The New Year picture of Yangliuqing in Tianjin employs the method of combing woodblock printing and hand painting, featuring multi-colors,

作，并用传统方式制作，题材广泛，想象力丰富，喜庆吉祥是其主题。在艺术特色方面喜浓墨重彩，构图完整匀称，造型粗壮朴实，线条简练流畅。

制作好的杨家埠年画——财神
A finished New Year picture of Yangjiabu type—The God of Wealth

　　四川绵竹年画以雕版艺术精湛、艺术情调高昂著称，讲求对称、完整、饱满，主次分明，色彩上采用对比手法，线条洗炼而流畅，刚柔结合，疏密有致，具有强烈的节奏感，而夸张且寓意丰富的造型更具诙谐活泼的效果，题材多反映社会生活场景。

　　年画艺术是中国社会历史、生活、信仰和风俗的反映，每逢农历新年时，人们都喜欢买年画贴在家里，有的家庭甚至从大门

绵竹年画——三喜童子
A New Year picture of Mianzhu type—Three Happy Children

a special human touch and life flavor. It has a wide range of subjects such as historical stories, myths, legends, opera figures, folk customs, landscapes, flowers and birds, among which opera figures, beautiful ladies and chubby children are the most exquisite and lifelike.

The New Year picture of Yangjiabu of Weifang City in Shandong Province is completely made with hands in a traditional way. With a wide range of subjects and rich imagination, its theme is happiness and good luck. Its artistic feature is thick and heavy colors, complete and well-balanced composition, sturdy and plain modeling, and simple and smooth lines.

The New Year picture of Mianzhu in Sichuan Province is well-known for its exquisite artistic skill and great artistic appeal. It emphasizes symmetry, completion, richness and distinction between the primary and the secondary parts. It uses the technique of contrast in choosing colors and prefers simple and smooth lines. The combination of hardness with softness and the proper density create a strong sense of rhythm. The exaggerated modeling with rich implications achieves the effect of amusement and vitality and the subjects of the picture mostly reflect scenes of social life.

The New Year picture reflects the history, life, belief, and customs in Chinese society. During the Spring Festival each year, people love to post New Year pictures up in their homes and in some families different-colored New Year pictures are seen everywhere from

到厅堂都贴满了各种花花绿绿、象征吉祥富贵的年画。新春佳节之所以充满欢乐热闹的气氛，年画起到了重要作用，更重要的是，它用直观可感的方式传承了我们的民族文化。

the front door to the hall to symbolize good fortune and wealth. New Year pictures play an important part in creating a happy and lively atmosphere during the Spring Festival. What is more important is that they also pass on our national culture in a direct and tangible way.

三言两语 A FEW REMARKS

清代晚期以来，到中国的外国人逐渐多起来，年画成了他们猎奇与收藏的一项重要内容。版画之乡荷兰的国家图书馆、热衷于收藏中国资料的德国莱比锡图书馆、为中国学研究服务的美国哈佛大学燕京图书馆，都专门藏有中国年画。外国人都这样对中国年画感兴趣，更不用说我们中国人了。

[中国] 赵岩，男，年画收藏家

Since the late Qing Dynasty, an increasing number of foreigners have been coming to China and the New Year picture is a novelty and an important collection for them. Chinese New Year pictures are also collected in the National Library of Netherlands which is home to block print, the German National Library Leipzig which is keen on collecting Chinese materials, and the Harvard-Yenching Library set up for Chinese studies. Foreigners are so interested in Chinese New Year pictures, let alone we Chinese people.
[China] Zhao Yan, male, New Year picture collector

早年间，杨柳青镇南三十六村家家户户都能做画，赶上旱涝不收的年景，画年画是这里乡亲维持生活的唯一途径。我画的缸鱼是专门贴在水缸上方的年画。阳光一照，墙上的鱼儿映在水中；一舀水，鱼儿随波游弋，栩栩如生，既好看又吉利，每到春节前夕，买的人可多了。

[中国] 王学勤，男，年画艺人

In early days, every family in the 36 villages in the south of the town of Yangliuqing were able to draw New Year pictures. If suffering from bad harvests due to drought or flood, the villagers' only way of making a living was to draw New Year pictures. I drew the New Year picture of fish that is specially pasted above the water vat. The fish on the wall are reflected in the water under the sunshine. If you take the water out of the vat, the fish seems to swim along with the wave, which is not only auspicious and good-looking but also as natural as though the fish were living. Every year before the Spring Festival, many people go to buy New Year pictures.
[China] Wang Xueqin, male, New Year picture artist

我在北京过过一次春节，没想到中国人过春节的气氛那么热烈。一位中国朋友邀请我去她家做客，我对她家里挂的色彩特别鲜艳的年画很感兴趣，尤其是一幅胖娃娃抱着大鱼坐在莲花上的年画，漂亮极了！朋友跟我说那是"连年有余"的意思，中国家庭都喜欢，不仅画面好看，还代表着美好的祝愿。

[加拿大] 安娜，女，大学生

I spent the Spring Festival in Beijing once and had never thought that the atmosphere of the festival would be so lively. A Chinese friend of mine invited me to her home. I took great interest in the bright-colored New Year pictures in her home, especially the extremely beautiful one depicting a chubby child sitting on the lotus and holding a big fish. My friend told me that the picture meant prosperity year after year and received much love from Chinese families due to its beauty and representation of good wishes.
[Canada] Anna, female, university student

版画是以"版"作为媒介来制作作品的一种绘画艺术，艺术家运用刀、笔或其他工具在石板、木板、金属板、塑料板等不同板材上绘制与雕刻，然后再经过印刷完成艺术作品。版画起源于印刷，最终又形成了自己独特的面貌。版画在历史上经历了由复制到创作两个阶段。早期版画的画者、刻者、印者相互分工，

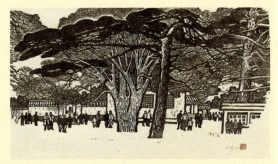

木刻版画《春游》，王琦作
Wood block print Spring Outing, made by Wang Qi

刻者只照画稿刻版，称复制版画；后来画刻印都由版画家一人来完成，使其艺术创造性得以发挥，称创作版画。中国复制木刻版画已有上千年历史，明清（1368—1911）达到高峰，出现了各种流派，创作出大量优秀作品。

Block print is a form of painting art which employs printing blocks as the means of producing painting works. Artists paint or carve with knives, pens or other tools on stales, wood blocks, metal plates and plastic blocks and then finish the art work after printing it. Stemming from printing and developing its own feature at last, block print has undergone two phases of history—duplication and creation. In the early stage, the painter, carver and printer of a block print were different persons and the carver only took the responsibility of carving the block based on the drawing, known as block-print duplication. Later, the work of block print was finished by only one person who was responsible for painting, carving and printing, which is known as block-print creation and in this way the artist's artistic creativity is given full play. Woodblock-print duplication in China has a history of thousands of years and reached its peak in the Ming and Qing dynasties (1368-1911) when various schools and enormous excellent works appeared.

Folk Sports 民间运动

毽 子

Shuttlecock

导入 INTRODUCTION

2004年11月28日，中国女子李汇凤以4小时37分的优异成绩创造了花毽盘踢吉尼斯世界纪录，成为世界上"持续踢毽时间最长的人"。此后她又于2006年12月24日在中央电视台《正大综艺》栏目举办的"挑战吉尼斯"节目中，以4小时40分的成绩再次创造了花毽盘踢吉尼斯世界纪录。

On November 28th, 2004, Li Huifeng, a Chinese female set the Guinness World Record for shuttlecock-kicking with a score of 4 hr 37 min non-stop, and thus becoming "the person who has the longest shuttlecock control with feet". In the TV program *Challenging Guinness* held during CCTV's *Zheng Da Variety Show* on December 24th, 2006, she reset the record with a score of 4 hr 40 min non-stop.

踢毽子起源于汉代（前206—公元220），盛行于南北朝（420—589）和隋唐（581—907），至今已有两千多年的历史了。明代（1368—1644）刘侗的《帝京景物略》中记载了一首北京儿童季节性活动的民谣："杨柳儿活，抽陀螺；杨柳儿青，放空钟；杨柳儿死，踢毽子。"可见在杨柳树落尽叶子的时候，气温最适宜于踢毽子。清代（1616—1911）末年踢花毽运动达到了顶峰，涌现出一大批踢毽高手，其中以谭俊川最为著名，人称"毽儿谭"。踢毽子发展到今天，已经成为中国最具特色、普及度最高的民间体育运动之一。

Originating in the Han Dynasty (206 BC-AD 220), prevailing through the Northern and Southern dynasties (420-589) and Sui Dynasty (581-907), shuttlecock-kicking has enjoyed a history of over two thousand years. In the book *Sketches of the Capital Landscapes* written by the Ming Dynasty (1368-1644) scholar Liu Dong, there is a piece of folk rhyme which goes "play spinning tops when willows wake up; toss diabolos when willows turn green; kick shuttlecocks when willows die". So we can see that when willows shed their final leaves, the temperature is the most suitable for kicking shuttlecocks. The sport of shuttlecock-kicking reached its climax in the late period of the Qing Dynasty (1616-1911) when a large number of shuttlecock masters emerged. Among them, Tan Junchuan was

羽毛毽
Shuttlecocks

踢毽子的基本动作有盘、拐、磕、绷四种。盘踢即用脚内侧踢，是踢毽子的基本功；拐踢是用脚外侧踢，能起到周转四方、远而往返的作用；磕踢是用膝盖将毽子向上弹起，对盘踢有辅助作用；绷踢即用脚尖正踢，是花样踢法的基础。若想成为踢毽子的高手，四种踢法缺一不可，在此基础上还可变

盘踢　*Pan-kicking*

换出更多的花样来。

毽子的花样踢法使踢毽子运动成为一种优美的技巧运动，一般分为接落、绕转、穿插、跳踢、头顶等几个

the most distinguished one and was referred to as Jian'er Tan by the public. At its present stage of development, shuttlecock-kicking has established itself as one of the most unique and popularized folk sports in China.

There are four basic movements used in kicking shuttlecocks, namely *pan*, *guai*, *ke* and *beng*. *Pan* is the basic skill of shuttlecock-kicking, which means people use the inner sides of their feet to kick the shuttlecock. *Guai* means kicking the shuttlecock with the outer sides of people's feet, which achieves the effect of adjusting the shuttlecock's direction and withdrawing it when it's moving further away from people's control. *Ke* is supplementary to *pan* and people employ their knees to propel the shuttlecock upward. As the foundation of free-style kicking, *beng* requires people to kick the shuttlecock with their tightly stretched tiptoes along the vertical direction. All of the four styles are indispensable for anyone hoping to become a

绷踢　*Beng-kicking*

master of shuttlecock-kicking. Based on these basic skills, people can make adaptations and create multiple new tricks.

Owing to its free-style kicking, shuttlecock-

相互关联的部分，由此又可派生出许多花样。各种花样踢法之间都有密切的联系，动作有大有小，有动有静，有前有后，有左有右，令人眼花缭乱、目不暇接，从而给人以赏心悦目之感。

除了娱乐以外，踢毽子也可以进行比赛。比赛有单人赛和集体赛，基本规则说起来简单做起来难，只要连续踢毽并使之不落，都可计数，越多越好。此外，还有一种团踢，即一群人共踢一个毽子，毽子落在谁面前，谁就可以任意选择踢法将毽子再次踢给其他人，毽子掉落在谁面前谁就输了。

团踢
Group kick

20世纪80年代中后期，毽球开始在中国亮相，成为一项新兴的体育项目。毽球由古老的民间踢毽子游戏

kicking has become a kind of exercise combining gracefulness and skills. The exercise can be divided into a number of related phases including catching the falling shuttlecock, circling and turning, switching to new tricks, jump kicking and overhead kicking, etc. Different types of free-style kicking are closely related: some feature large-scale movements while others only require minor motions; some are dynamic while others static; some require front-kicking while others back-kicking; some focus on left-kicking while others on right-kicking. All these brilliant tricks seem too many for people to appreciate at one time, which makes people dazzled and captures their minds as well as pleases their eyes.

Apart from being a form of entertainment, shuttlecock-kicking can also be used in competitions. The competition consists of single kicks and group kicks whose basic rules are simple but hard to fulfill. Each kick can be counted as long as a person kicks continuously without letting the shuttlecock touch the ground. The more kicks the better. In addition, there is another form called group kick in which a group of people kick the same shuttlecock. When the shuttlecock reaches in front of someone, he or she can choose whatever methods they like to kick the shuttlecock to another person. The fall of the shuttlecock onto the ground in front of a person indicates the failure of that particular person.

In the middle and late years of the 1980s, shuttlecock established itself as a new sport

演变而来，并在花毽趣味性、观赏性、健身性的基础上增加了对抗性，集羽毛球的场地、排球的规则、足球的技术为一体，是一种隔网相争的体育项目。

which gradually appeared in China. The sport shuttlecock evolved from ancient folk shuttlecock-kicking. It added a confrontation orientation to the entertainment, along with the appreciation and fitness-building nature of free-style shuttlecock-kicking. Using a badminton court as the playground, the sport combines specifications of volleyball with skills needed in basketball, and became a sport activity in which two parties compete on separate sides of a net.

毽球比赛　*Shuttlecock competition*

踢毽子对身心健康极为有益。经常参加此项活动不仅可使肌肉、韧带富有弹性，关节灵活，而且可以使心肺系统得到全面锻炼，起到增进身心健康的良好作用。

Kicking shuttlecock is highly beneficial for people's physical and mental health. For people who frequently participate in this exercise, they will not only develop more resilient muscles and ligaments and flexible joints, but also comprehensively strengthen their cardiopulmonary system which will eventually bring them benefits such as boosting their physical and mental health.

　　我小时候最喜欢踢毽子了，每天课间都要跟小伙伴们玩儿一会儿。那时候的娱乐项目不多，大家也就是在一起跳跳皮筋、跨跨方格、踢踢毽子什么的，快乐来得很简单。我记得当时班里有好些身手灵活的同学，能把毽子踢出很多花样，可让人羡慕了。

[中国] 宋红燕，女，国家公务员

Kicking shuttlecocks was my favorite exercise in childhood. During class breaks, I would play it for a while with my friends. Back then, there were only a few recreational activities. So children just gathered together to play rubber band, cross squares drawn on the ground and kick the shuttlecock. It seemed that happiness was so easy to experience. I still remember that some flexible classmates could kick the shuttlecock applying different tricks. I admired them so much.

[China] Song Hongyan, female, national civil servant

　　毽球是一项非常出色的运动，它讲究技术、不受时间空间的限制，什么人都可以玩儿，每个人都可以选择适合自己的档次，又不像足球那样容

Shuttlecock is a kind of extraordinary sport for it stresses the use of skills and is not confined by

易有身体上的碰撞和损伤。如果你是害羞的，你可以躲在家里自己练，过一阵水平提高了，你就可以站出来说自己是高手。到了一定的水平，你会自觉地跟别人围起来切磋一下，逐渐有了合作伙伴，这样，性格很内向的人也会有新朋友。

[德国] 皮特，男，毽球教练

time and space. Everyone can play it by choosing from their individual levels; besides, it is free of the physical conflicts and injuries which may easily occur while playing football. If you are a shy person, you can start practicing in your home. After you've made improvements to your skills, you can demonstrate yourself as a master in public. When you reach a certain level, you will consciously share and exchange understandings with other players. In this way, you will gradually find partners and make new friends even when you are an introvert.

[Germany] Peter, male, shuttlecock coach

小链接 ADDITIONAL INFORMATION

极限飞盘是一项以飞盘为对象、严格避免选手之间身体接触的比赛项目，1967年始创于美国，现在已经发展成为一项融汇了许多运动特点的团队竞赛项目。玩者可通过各种战术方式的跑动、传递飞盘，让自己的队友在得分区接盘达阵，从而得分。为了赢得比赛，参与的选手必须具备良好的体能、迅捷的速度、敏锐的判断以及高超的控盘技巧。有人曾对极限飞盘运动下过这样的定义：极限飞盘=飞盘+足球的耐力折返跑+美式足球的得分方式。

极限飞盘比赛 *Ultimate frisbee competition*

Ultimate frisbee is a sport competition which uses a frisbee as target and strictly prohibits body contact between players. Invented in 1967 in America, ultimate frisbee has developed into a team competition event combining characteristics of various sports. Players can run and pass on the frisbee using multiple kinds of tactics to let their team members catch the frisbee and advance it to the scoring zone. Substantial physical strength, swift movements, acute senses and superior frisbee-controlling skills are essential for players intending to win the competition. Someone once gave ultimate frisbee such a definition: ultimate frisbee = frisbee + endurance required in running back and forth while playing football + scoring methods of American soccer.

风 筝
Chinese Kite

2012年是龙年，农历二月初二民间俗称"龙抬头"，在这个传统节日里，太原数百名风筝爱好者齐放龙形风筝，其中最大的是"八卦龙"。据该风筝的主人宁磊介绍，这条龙长达61米，耗时11天制作而成。太原有龙城之称，龙年在龙城放飞龙筝更有一种特殊意义，即希望龙城太原在龙年能够像龙一样飞腾。

龙筝 *A dragon kite*

2012 is the year of the dragon. In the traditional Chinese calendar, February 2nd is the day when "the dragon raises his head". On this traditional festival, hundreds of kite lovers from Taiyuan City would gather together to fly dragon kites among which a "*bagua* dragon" (a dragon-shaped kite with trigram patterns) is the biggest one. According to its owner Ning Lei, he spent eleven days to produce the 61-meter long dragon kite. Taiyuan City is referred to as the city of the dragon, thus flying dragon kites in the dragon city in the year of the dragon carries a special significance: wishing Taiyuan City to prosper as the dragon in the year 2012.

中国人放风筝已有两千多年的历史。据《韩非子·外储说》记载，墨翟居鲁山（今山东青州一带），"斫木为鹞，三年而成飞一日而败"。这里是说墨子用三年时间制成了一只木鸟，但只飞了一天就坏了，这可以说是中国最早的风筝了。风筝最初用于传递书信，隋唐（581—907）时人

China has over 2000 years' history of kite flying. As recorded in "Waichushuo" from the ancient book *Han Feizi*, Mo Di, a Chinese philosopher who lived on Lushan Mountain (roughly in today's Qingzhou area in Shandong Province), "斫木为鹞，三年而成飞一日而败" (Mo Di spent three years to construct a wooden bird; however it broke down after only one day's flight). The wooden

们开始用纸裱糊风筝，宋代（960—1279）放风筝成为人们喜爱的户外休闲娱乐活动，元代（1206—1368）意大利人马可·波罗把风筝介绍到了西方。

以风筝为主题的艺术品
A work of art with kites as its theme

　　中国风筝讲究寓意吉祥：运用人物、走兽、花鸟、器物等形象和一些吉祥文字，通过借喻、比拟、双关、象征及谐音等表现手法，构成"一句吉语一图案"的美术形式，寄托人们

不同样式的风筝　*Kites with different styles*

bird is regarded as the earliest kite in China. The kite was originally used to send letters and messages. Later in the Sui and Tang dynasties (581-907), people began to make kites with paper. In the Song Dynasty (960-1279), flying kites became one of people's favorite outdoor entertainments. Later in the Yuan Dynasty (1206-1368), an Italian named Marco Polo introduced kites into the western world.

Chinese kites emphasize the expression of auspicious connotations. Symbols such as people, quadrupeds, flowers, birds, implements are combined with auspicious Chinese characters. By utilizing rhetorical devices such as metonymy, parallel, pun, symbolism and homophony, these symbols and characters achieve an artistic form featuring "a lucky remark and one beautiful pattern", which expresses people's dream for a happy life. Auspicious Chinese patterns are rich in styles. Generally there are the following styles, namely "praying for happiness", "offering birthday congratulations", "celebrating happy events" and "practicing divination for good marriage", etc.

Praying for happiness: this is related to people's common psychology of pursuing happiness. Because of the fact that "蝙蝠 biānfú" (bat) is homophonous to "遍福 biàn fú" (happiness surrounding everywhere) and "遍富 biàn fù" (wide-spread wealth) and that

美好的生活愿望。中国吉祥图案内容丰富，大体有"求福"、"祝寿"、"庆喜"、"纳吉"等类型。

求福：这与人们对幸福有共同的追求心理有关。因"蝙蝠"与

翅膀上画有蝙蝠图案的风筝
A kite with bat patterns on its wings

"遍福"、"遍富"谐音，又有翅膀可以飞翔，故蝙蝠是最常用的象征"福"的吉祥图案。

祝寿：风筝中的松柏、仙鹤、灵芝、仙桃等图案都可以寄寓和祝颂长寿，与此有关的吉祥图案有"祥云鹤寿"、"八仙贺寿"等。

庆喜："囍"是人们常见的喜庆图案，喜鹊也是喜事的征兆，与此有关的吉祥图案有"喜上眉梢"、"双喜登眉"、"喜庆有余"等。此外，百蝶、百鸟、百花、百吉、百寿、百福等图案也可用于庆喜。

纳吉：龙、凤、麒麟是人们想象中的瑞禽仁兽，龙被视为中华古老文明的象征，凤是百鸟之王，麒麟能带来好运，因此，以此构成的传统吉祥图案有"龙凤呈祥"、"二龙

bats have wings to fly, bat patterns become the most commonly used ones to symbolize "happiness".

Offering birthday congratulations: patterns of pine and cypress, crane, ganodorma lucidum and peach all incorporate connotations of longevity. Designs related these symbols are "auspicious clouds and cranes symbolizing long life" and "the Eight Immortals offering birthday congratulations", etc.

Celebrating happy events: "囍" is a lucky pattern commonly seen by people, and the magpie is also an omen of happiness. Related auspicious patterns include "喜上眉梢" (delight shown in one's eyebrows), "双喜登眉" (two lucky events arriving on somebody) and "喜庆有余" (overflowing happiness), etc. Besides these, there are also other patterns used to symbolize happiness, such as butterflies, birds, flowers and the characters "吉" (auspiciousness), "寿" (longevity) and "福" (happiness).

Practicing divination for good marriage: the dragon, phoenix and Chinese unicorn are imagined birds or animals symbolizing good luck and benevolence. The dragon is regarded as a sign of the ancient Chinese civilization, and the phoenix queen of all birds, moreover the Chinese unicorn can bring people good luck; so traditional auspicious patterns formed by these birds or animals include "the dragon and phoenix indicating auspicious

omen", "two dragons circulating the pearl", "two colorful phoenixes flying side by side", "hundreds of birds worshipping the phoenix", "Chinese unicorns sending people children as gifts", etc.

There is an old saying in China which goes as "鸢者长寿", meaning people who fly kites live longer lives. While fixing their gazes on the kites soaring above the clouds in the blue sky, people become devoid of distracting considerations and forget about all the confinements of earthly life as honor and disgrace. When flying kites, people have to run here and there, which enhances their cardiopulmonary health and boosts metabolism and eventually achieves the effect of retaining people's health and extending their lifespan.

有龙纹图案的风筝　*A kite with patterns of dragon*

戏珠"、"彩凤双飞"、"百鸟朝凤"、"麒麟送子"等。

中国有句古话："鸢者长寿"，即放风筝的人长寿。双目凝视于蓝天白云之上的飞鸢，杂念俱无，荣辱皆忘，而跑来跑去又可增强心肺功能，促进新陈代谢，达到健康长寿的目的。

无论南鹞北鸢，风筝均讲究诗情画意。曹雪芹认为风筝是"环境艺术"与"动感艺术"的有机结合，更让我敬佩的是这位大师的才情与仁义。当年他教残疾人以风筝技艺谋生，而现在我的师傅孔令民在北京上庄的"曹氏风筝工艺坊"即是传承曹雪芹先生当年的做法，帮助弱势人群，同时也能将风筝传统技艺传播开来。

[中国] 缪伯刚，男，"风筝曹"
第四代传承人

No matter in the north or south, the art of kites emphasizes poetic beauty. Cao Xueqin believed that the kite is an organic integration of "the art of setting" and "the art of movements". I particularly admire the master's brilliant expression of emotions and kindheartedness and justice. He once taught the physically handicapped to make a living by kite skills. Now, what my teacher Kong Lingmin is doing in his Cao's Kite Craft Workshop based in Shangzhuang in Beijing is exactly an inheritance of Cao Xueqin's practice. He aims at helping disadvantaged people as well as spreading traditional kite crafts.

[China] Miao Bogang, male, the fourth-generation inheritor of Cao's Kites

风筝是伊朗小朋友的宝贝。小时候的我，当早上的第一缕阳光从东方

The kite is a kind of treasure among Iranian children. When I was young, I would go outside and fly kites

升起来时，就出门跟一群小朋友放风筝。天上的风筝告诉我们：生活充满了坎坷，有时可以飞得很高，有时也许只能飞得很低，但是永远不要失去希望，只要努力，只要认真，只要奋斗就可以像风筝一样飞向阳光。我们应该感谢起源于中国的风筝，它给世界上的小朋友们带来了无比的快乐与生活的启示。

[伊朗] 穆斯塔法，男，研究生

with my friends as the first glow of the sun rose from the east. The kites in the sky told us that life is full of obstacles. Sometimes we can soar very high but sometimes we can only hover near the ground. However, we should never lose our hope. As long as we work hard, appear conscientious and strive for our goals, we will be able to fly to the sunlight just as the kite does. We should really thank kites that originated in China, for they bring children all over the world unparalleled happiness and enlightenment for life.

[Iran] Mustafa, male, graduate student

小链接 ADDITIONAL INFORMATION

马来西亚人喜欢放风筝，据说是为了向稻神致意。在马来西亚有这样一个传说：很久以前，有个庄稼汉在田里遇到一个迷路的女孩，就把她带回家抚养。女孩越长越漂亮，他和乡亲们的收成也越来越好。谁知他老婆起了妒忌之心，把女孩赶出了家门，从此村子里的收成越来越差，原来那位姑娘是稻神。后来有人告诉他，必须做一个漂亮的东西，放到空中稻神所在之处，向她表示忏悔，收成才会好起来。这个庄稼汉便做了风筝放到空中，人们的日子又富裕起来了。

马来西亚风筝　*A Malaysian kite*

Malaysians are fond of flying kites, which was said to be a tribute given to the goddess of paddy. According to a Malaysian folklore, a long time ago, a male peasant came across a girl who had lost her way in the field, thus he took the girl home and raised her. As the girl was growing to be more and more beautiful, the peasants were getting better and better harvests. However, the peasant's wife became jealous of the girl's beauty thus she drove the girl away. Since then, the village suffered from poorer and poorer harvests, for the girl was the goddess of paddy. Later on, someone told the peasant that he had to make a beautiful object and send it to the heaven where the goddess resides so as to show his regret. Only by doing this could they harvest better results in the future. The peasant made kites and flew them into the sky, which again brought people a wealthy life.

武术—器械术
Martial Arts–Weapon Wielding

导入 INTRODUCTION

电影《卧虎藏龙》剧照
Still from the film Crouching Tiger, Hidden Dragon

中国电影《卧虎藏龙》[1]用艺术的手法让世界各国的人们更加了解了中国功夫，故事情节是围绕一把青龙剑展开的，影片中的"剑术"都属于武术中的器械术。《时代周刊》（TIME）著名影评人理查德·西凯尔（Richard Corliss）称《卧虎藏龙》有着很好的艺术性，对人之间的感情有着很好的阐述，不同于以往的"kicks ass"功夫片一味强调"打架"。[2]

The Chinese film *Crouching Tiger, Hidden Dragon*[1] enables people of different countries in the world to better understand Chinese kungfu by the successful employment of artistic skills. The story unfolds around a Qinglong Sword (green dragon sword), and the swordplay presented in the film all belongs to weapon wielding. Richard Corliss, a famous film critic of *Time* magazine praised the film for its excellent artistic value and elaborate depiction of the love between the two main characters, which is distinct from those former "kicks ass" kungfu films focusing invariably on "fighting".[2]

中华武术分为拳术和器械术，"十八般武艺"则是指武术对十八种兵器的使用。十八种兵器一般是指刀、枪、剑、戟、斧、钺、钩、叉、鞭、锏、锤、抓、镋、棍、槊、棒、拐、流星锤。

Chinese martial arts are classified into boxing and weapon wielding, and "*shiba ban wuyi*" refers to the wielding of 18 kinds of weapons. The 18 weapons generally include saber, spear, straight sword, halberd, axe, battle axe, hook sword, trident, chain whip, mace, hammer,

[1] 该片获得2001年奥斯卡最佳外语片等四项奖项。
[2] 此评论来自2012年5月17日《时代周刊》理查德·西凯尔（Richard Corliss）的影评文章《本世纪最伟大的十部电影》。

[1] The film won the Academy Award for Best Foreign Language Film and three other Academy Awards in 2011.
[2] The comment originally appeared in Richard Corliss's film review "The 10 Greatest Movies of the Millennium" published in *Time* magazine on May 17th, 2012.

十八般兵器　*The 18 main weapons in Chinese martial arts*

武术中的器械大致可分为短兵器、长兵器、软兵器三类，最常用的当属刀、剑、枪、棍、鞭五种。

短兵器一般不超过常人的眉际，分量较轻，使用时可单手握持，以刀和剑最为常见。刀的套路有单刀和双刀两种：单刀要求勇猛迅疾，势如破竹；而双刀则更富于观赏性，舞起来

刀与剑　*Saber and sword*

talon, trident-halberd, staff, long-handled spear, cudgel, crutch, meteor hammer.

Weapons used in martial arts roughly fall into three categories: short weapons, long weapons and soft weapons. The most commonly used weapons include saber, sword, spear, staff and chain whip.

Usually, short weapons will not exceed the length measuring from an average person's feet to his eyebrow; they are particularly lighter and can be held by a single hand. The most commonly seen short weapons are saber and sword. There are two types of saber skills, namely single-saber skills and double-saber skills. The former requires powerful and swift motions as splitting a piece of bamboo with crushing force. The latter, however, comes with higher artistic value; for its performance resembles a rolling mass of snow and the performer can hardly be recognized. Swords emerged no later than the Shang Dynasty. Famous swords include the Longquan Sword (the dragon spring sword), the Qinglong Sword (the green dragon sword) and the Qingshe Sword (the green snake sword) and so on. The art of swordplay consists of splitting, piercing,

如团雪翻滚，不见人影。剑至迟出现在殷商时期，著名的有龙泉剑、青龙剑、青蛇剑等。剑的基本技法有劈、刺、撩、抹、斩等，敏捷而飘逸，故有"刀如猛虎，剑如飞凤"之说。

长兵器多高于人体，如枪、棍等。枪是一种长柄的刺击兵器，由古代的矛演变而来，枪法主要有扎、刺、拦、扑、拨等。枪术不易掌握，俗话说："年拳，月棒，久练枪。"棍是人类最早使用的防卫器具之一，有少林棍、青田棍等派别，练棍可以提高练习者手、眼、身、法、步的协调与配合。

少林棍表演
Shaolin staff performance

软兵器泛指各种以环、链和绳索为中间环节串连而成的器械，如三节棍、九节鞭等。三节棍使用时轻巧方便，可近可远，可方可圆，可伸可缩。与三节棍相比，双节棍则更短小精巧。不用时别在衣服里面作防身武器。九节鞭每节之间用三个圆环连接，

lifting, wiping and cutting which all appear swift and graceful, hence the saying "sabers are like ferocious tigers while swords like soaring phoenixes".

Long weapons are generally taller than human, such as spears and staffs. As a piercing weapon with long shaft, the spear evolved from ancient lance. The skills of spear-wielding mainly include pricking, piercing, blocking, pouncing and stirring, etc. These skills are not easy to grasp, as the saying goes "it takes a year to master boxing, a month to cudgel whereas long years to spear". Staff is one of the earliest weapons used by humans to defend themselves. There are different sects of staff such as Shaolin and Qingtian, etc. People can improve the coordination of their hands, eyes, body, skills and paces by exercising with staffs.

Soft weapons generally refer to weapons joined by all kinds of rings, chains or ropes, such as the three-section staff and the nine-section chain whip. The three-section staff is light and convenient to use; it can reach near and far, form a square or a circle, and stretch out and draw back. Compared with three-section staff, a two-section staff is shorter and delicate and can be put in the pocket as a weapon of self-defense. Each rod of a nine-section chain whip is linked to another by three rings; a circle capable of producing a rushing sound is attached to the ring in the middle. A piece of red cloth is tied to the dart at one end of the whip, and a green cloth to the handle at the other. This adds visual appeal while the whip swings through the air, and serves a function of adjusting the movement of the whip.

中间还有响环，鞭头常拴一块红色的彩绸，鞭把拴一块绿色的彩绸，舞动起来非常美观，且具有调整舞动路线的功用。

九节鞭
Nine-section chain whip

　　武术既可以用来强身健体，也可用来保家卫国，无论用于何处，习武之人都要把武德放在首要位置，讲究"武以德立"、"德为艺先"，且《左传》中有"止戈为武"之说——"武"字是"止"、"戈"两字合成的，所以止战才是真正的武功。能够不用武力化干戈为玉帛，才是武术的最高境界。

Martial arts can not only be used as a means of strengthening the body, but also a tool of protecting homes and defending the country. No matter what their expectations are, practitioners of martial arts should give number one priority to "martial morality" and observe the ethics of "martial arts building upon morality" and "morality coming before skills". Moreover, according to the saying "止戈为武" set in the book *Chronicle of Zuo*, the word "武" is a combination of the two characters "止" and "戈", which means stopping the use of weapons and avoiding war is truly martial arts. Being able to cease hostilities and negotiate for peace without resorting to weapons is the ultimate state of martial arts.

三言两语 A FEW REMARKS

　　2001年我第一次接触双节棍，那时还没有什么学习视频，我只能看着李小龙的电影自己摸索着练习。李小龙的双节棍动作实用且简单，但我不想满足于这些现有的动作，于是就和朋友着手研究双节棍的新招式。后来我开办了双节棍俱乐部，我的目标就是大力推广双节棍运动，让大家都拿起双节棍来强身健体。

　　[中国] 徐守波，男，双节棍教练

When I first knew of the two-section staff, there were few videos teaching how to use it, so I could only imitate Bruce Lee while watching his movies. Bruce Lee's two-section staff technique is simple yet practical, but I was not satisfied with the existing skills, so I started working on new tricks with my friends. Before long, I established a two-section staff club aiming at promoting the exercise and encouraging people to strengthen their health using the staff.

[China] Xu Shoubo, male, coach of two-section staff

习武，器械术必不可少。清代武术家吴殳说："历代武术名家皆以兵器技艺服人，而不在拳术上论高下。"作为一个武术爱好者，不学点儿器械术怎么能了解武功的真谛呢？

[中国] 高强，男，武术爱好者

The manipulation of weapons is essential to anyone who practices martial arts. As the Qing Dynasty martial artist Wu Shu said "those distinguished martial artists all impress people with the skills of wielding weapons instead of competing for better boxing techniques." As a lover of martial arts, how can we understand the true meaning of it without learning some weapon-wielding skills?

[China] Gao Qiang, male, martial arts lover

我从小就想学中国功夫，但一直没有机会，来到中国后又觉得很难，怕学不好。功夫就是中国的武术，在世界上是第一流的。学功夫有很多好处，不仅能保护自己，还可以让自己更有信心和勇气，我想以后我会下决心学习中国功夫的。

[苏丹] 哈默图，男，大学生

I've been dreaming of learning Chinese kungfu since my childhood, yet I couldn't find a chance. When I came to China later, I was afraid that I can't learn it well for it is too hard. Kungfu. the martial art of China is among the world's first-class techniques. I can benefit a lot from learning kungfu. I can not only defend myself but also build up my confidence and foster my bravery. I think I'll make up my mind in learning Chinese kungfu in the near future.

[Republic of Sudan] Hamoto, male, college student

小链接 ADDITIONAL INFORMATION

1965年，湖北江陵望山 1 号墓出土了著名的越王勾践剑。此剑由青铜铸造，正面用蓝色琉璃、背面用绿松石嵌出美丽的花纹，整个剑身满饰菱形暗纹，在靠近剑格的地方刻有鸟篆体错金铭文"越王鸠潜，自乍用剑"①八个字，字迹非常清楚。此剑至今剑锋犀利，寒光闪闪，出土时插于漆木鞘里，保存完好，至今犹能断发。经科学分析测定，剑脊含锡低，为10%，韧性好而不易折断；刃部含锡高，为20%，坚硬而锋利。此剑堪称剑器精品中的精品。

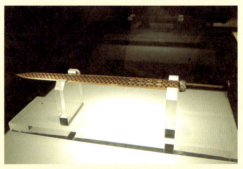

越王勾践剑（湖北省博物馆藏）
The Sword of Goujian (preserved in Hubei Provincial Museum)

①越王鸠潜，自乍用剑："鸠潜"即"勾践"，"乍"即"作"。

In 1965, a renowned sword, The Sword of Goujian (the King of Yue Kingdom during the Spring and Autumn Period) was excavated from Wangshan site No.1 in Jiangling County, Hubei Province. Cast from bronze, the front side of the sword is ornamented with patterns of inlaid blue crystals, and the back side with embedded turquoise. Repeating dark rhombus patterns cover both sides of the blade. On the blade near the handle, there are eight gold-inlaid characters written in clear bird-worm seal script saying "越王鸠潜，自乍用剑"[1] (King of Yue made this sword for personal use). Upon discovery, the sword was found sheathed in a wooden scabbard finished in black lacquer; it is well-preserved and remains sharp and shiny till this day. According to scientific examination, the central ridge contains a low percentage of tin (10%), making it more pliant and less likely to shatter; the edges have more tin content (20%), making them harder and sharper. The sword is indisputably one of the best of its kind.

---

[1] 越王鸠潜，自乍用剑: "鸠潜" refers to Goujian, "乍" is another form of "作" (make).

秧 歌

Yangge

2004年1月24日，"北京风情舞动巴黎"——中法文化年、北京文化周盛装游行在法国巴黎著名的香榭丽舍大街隆重举行，这是东方人的舞姿第一次出现在这条浪漫古典的风情大道上。秧歌表演团的演员们身着绣有中国民俗图案的传统服饰，手持花棍，踏着京剧锣鼓点，扭着秧歌走在香榭丽舍大街上。

中国秧歌队走在巴黎香榭丽舍大街上
Procession of a Chinese yangge troupe on the Champs-Elysees in Paris

On January 24th, 2004, a pageant known as the Beijing Style Dancing in Paris which was part of the Sino-France Culture Year, Beijing Culture Week, was ceremoniously held on the Champs-Elysees in Paris. The occasion marked the debut of an oriental dancing on the romantic and classical avenue. Dressed in traditional costumes embroidered with designs of Chinese folk custom while holding sticks decorated with flowers, dancers of the *yangge* troupe walked to the gong and drum sound of Peking opera and performed *yangge* on the Champs-Elysees.

秧歌是流行于中国北方地区的一种民间舞蹈形式，男女老少都可以在锣鼓、唢呐等乐器的伴奏下扭起生动活泼、多姿多彩的秧歌，表达自己对生活的热爱。

秧歌起源于插秧耕田的劳动生活，又和古代祭祀农神、祈福禳灾有关。它在发展过程中不断地吸收杂

Yangge is a form of folk dance popular in northern China. Males and females of different ages are able to perform the lively and colorful *yangge* with the accompaniment of such musical instruments as gongs and *suona*s (woodwind instrument resembling a trumpet). By doing this, they are expressing their enthusiasm for life.

Originating from rice-transplanting and land

技、戏曲等技艺与形式，发展成为一种独特的民间歌舞。清代（1616—1911）秧歌在中国广泛流传，目前秧

扭秧歌　*Yangge performance*

歌主要见于东北、西北、华北地区。

　　秧歌表演场面宏大，气氛热烈，主要有以下几个特点：

　　一是"扭"。秧歌重跳不重唱，最常见的是"十字步"，动作依次为左脚迈向右前方、右脚迈向左前方、左脚向左后方撤一步、右脚向右后方撤一步。如此循环往复，手臂随着脚步相反的方向摆动，这样就走出来一个"十字步"，身体也就自然扭动起来了。

　　二是"走场"。走场分为大场和小场。大场是边走边舞的各种队形组合的大型集体舞，小场则是由两人或三人表演的带有简单情节的舞蹈小戏。一般在秧歌开始和结束时走的是

cultivation, *yangge* is also related to the ancient practice of offering sacrifices to the god of agriculture in the hope of ushering in good fortunes and averting misfortunes. In its development, *yangge* consistently absorbed such skills and forms as acrobatics and opera, and eventually evolved to a distinctive form of folk dance. In the Qing Dynasty (1616-1911), *yangge* was widely spread in China. Now *yangge* is primarily seen in northeast, northwest and northern China.

Yangge performance features grand scale and lively atmosphere. Its characteristics are summarized as follows:

The first is "swing". *Yangge* emphasizes dancing rather than singing. The most common movement is called the "cross-step" in which a dancer moves his or her feet in the following order: stretch the left foot to the right front direction, then the right foot to the left front direction; then withdraw the left foot for a step to the left rear direction and then the right foot to the right rear direction. The movements are repeated with the hands swinging in directions opposite to that of the step, forming a "cross-step" movement which naturally sets the body swinging.

The second is "staging". Staging can be either grand or small. Grand staging refers to large-scale group dances consisting of various walk-and-dance formations. Small staging refers to

大场，中间穿插小场。

　　三是"扮"。扭秧歌时要穿专门的服装甚至化妆，服装色彩对比很强烈，妆也化得很浓艳。有时手里持花扇，有时腰里系红绸。若是表演历史故事，还会扮成公子、少妇、渔翁、丑婆、货郎、孩童等。

二人扮的小场　　*Small staging of a duet*

　　中国秧歌以东北地区和陕北地区最具代表性。东北秧歌风格诙谐，鼓点节奏十分明快，追求稳中浪、浪中梗、梗中翘。陕北秧歌风格豪放，因而有"闹秧歌"之说。秧歌表演者常有数十人，在"伞头"——手持伞头的表演者，一般是秧歌队的统

陕北安塞地区的秧歌
Yangge performance in Ansai County of northern Shaanxi Province

minor dancing plays featuring simple plots performed by two or three artists. Grand staging usually occurs at the commencement or termination of *yangge* performances while small staging is interspersed in between.

The third is "make-up". While performing *yangge*, dancers dress in special costumes with striking contrast of colors and even while putting on heavy make-up. At times, they hold colorful dancing fans in their hands or tie red silk ribbons around their waists. In the case of a historical story performance, dancers will dress up as childes, maidens, fishermen, female clowns, peddlers and children, etc.

Among various forms of Chinese *yangge*, those in northeastern China and northern Shaanxi Province are the most representative ones. The northeastern *yangge* possesses a strong taste of humor and comes with lively and quick rhythm of drums; it seeks the aims of exuberance amidst steadiness, vigorous swing amid liveliness, and raising bodies while swinging. *Yangge* of northern Shaanxi Province has a bold and uninhibited nature, hence the saying "messing about while dancing *yangge*". A *yangge* troupe usually consists of dozens of performers dancing passionately to the sonorous sound made by gongs and *suonas* under the leadership of a chief performer called *santou* who holds an umbrella in his or her hands.

领——的带领下，踏着铿锵的锣鼓、和着嘹亮的唢呐尽情欢舞。

扭秧歌全身都要动起来，是一项男女老少皆宜的健身运动。除了健身功效外，极具表演特色的秧歌如今还登上了各种剧场的舞台，成为一种雅俗共赏的节目。

While performing *yangge*, people have to move every part of their bodies, thus rendering the dance an exercise suitable for males and females of different ages. Apart from its health effects, *yangge* has presented itself on the stages of all kinds of theaters by virtue of its superior degree of performability and established itself as a program catering to both refined and popular tastes.

在陕北，每年正月十五都要举行秧歌会演。每到这个时候，大街小巷回荡着粗犷而欢快的锣鼓声，不用说，这就是秧歌的伴奏了。浩浩荡荡的数十个秧歌队，如阅兵般自天而来。又是拜年，又是会演，加上老百姓熙熙攘攘地围绕在秧歌队周围，街道上空几天都升腾着节日的愉悦气氛。

[中国] 依洛河，男，技术员

我很喜欢中国的秧歌，因为它有欢快的音乐、艳丽的服装和自由的动作。每当看到大街上和公园里有人扭秧歌时，我就会想起我们古巴的舞蹈，中国的秧歌和古巴的舞蹈当然不一样，但有一点是共同的，就是它们谁都可以表演，随时随地都可以表演，或者说根本就不是为了表演，而是为了自己高兴。

[古巴] 埃丽萨，女，大学生

In northern Shaanxi Province, *yangge* performances are held each year on the 15th day of the lunar New Year. At this time of the year, the streets and alleys reverberate with sonorous and cheerful sound made by gongs and drums, which is obviously the accompaniment of *yangge*. A massive procession comprising dozens of *yangge* troupes emerge on the streets as if it were a troop sent from heaven. On this occasion, people offer New Year greetings to each other and organize *yangge* performances. The troupes are surrounded by huge crowds of people and the streets are filled with a festive atmosphere lingering on for days.

[China] Yi Luohe, male, technician

I really like Chinese *yangge*, because it has cheerful music, colorful costumes and free movements. I would think of our Cuban dances whenever I see people dancing *yangge* on the streets or in the parks. It is apparent that Chinese *yangge* is different from Cuban dances, nevertheless, they have one point in common, that is both of them can be performed by anyone at any place. To put it more precisely, dancing is not for performance but self-entertainment.

[Cuba] Elisa, female, college student

绘画中的古巴舞蹈，田琨摄
*Cuban dance represented in a painting,
photographed by Tian Kun*

古巴国际舞蹈节是一年一度的国际舞蹈盛会，世界各国的舞蹈者带来了最具本国文化特点的舞蹈。舞蹈节没有固定的演出场所，哈瓦那的老街道就是舞台，在这个开放的大舞台上，各国表演者将本民族最优秀的舞蹈文化呈现在人们眼前，让观者大饱眼福，原本就迷人的哈瓦那也因为这些舞者的出现增添了动感与活力。古巴国际舞蹈节是世界上最重要的舞蹈节之一，它促进了各个国家与民族舞蹈乃至文化的交流，使舞蹈这种艺术形式更加贴近大众。

Held annually, the Cuba International Dance Festival is a grand international dance event in which dancers from different countries of the world present dances most unique to their own cultures. There is no fixed venue for the festival; hence the old streets in Havana readily serve as the stage. On this grand and open stage, performers of various countries present their best national dance cultures to spectators feasting their eyes on rich forms of dancing. Owing to the presence of these dancers, the already charming Havana is flavored with a sense of vigor and vitality. As one of the world's most important dance festivals, the Cuba International Dance Festival has been promoting the exchange between different countries in aspects of national dance or even culture, thus rendering dancing closer to the public as a form of art.